# The Backside of God

—⁂—

## *and Other Sermons*

*(including six new sermons)*

+John S. Thornton

ISBN: 1535189215

ISBN: 9781535189217

For permissions or reprint information,
please contact jsthornton32@gmail.com

Edited by Stuart Hotchkiss

Front cover painting by Cornelia Wattley

Printed in the USA

# Table of Contents

# Dedication

*This book is dedicated to our parents,*

*Andrew Robertson Thornton*

*Gertrude Mae (Nicol) Thornton*

*William DeBoer*

*Dorothy Amelia (Muyskens) DeBoer*

# Introduction

This is a collection of eleven sermons. One was preached at St. Mary's, Eugene, Oregon, one at St. Thomas, Ketchum, Idaho and one at St. Barnabas on the Desert, Scottsdale, Arizona. All the rest were preached at St. Michael's Cathedral, Boise, Idaho.

I haven't arranged the sermons chronologically or, really, logically in any way. I haven't, deliberately, arranged them thematically. You may find a theme – or several of them – as you read along. If you do, you'll find the theme(s) of my preaching and teaching now that I'm beyond the years of striving. The arrangement is what suits me, that's all. The collection begins with "The Backside of God" and ends with "Namaan." In between are nine sermons even I enjoy re-reading.

I find the orthodoxy of the Church very satisfying, though, in my continuing study of the New Testament and Christian theologians, I'm still trying to figure out what it is beyond my firm belief that Jesus of Nazareth was and is the Risen Human Being. But I also think that the Trinity is the model for all personal relationships, in which "none is afore, or after other; none is greater, or less than another." Oh, and I have little trouble imagining the Church as the Body of Christ, though it's definitely shy about getting crucified. Anyway, I'm not a rebel.

I have my own storytelling style, I've been told. I have my own sense of humor too, and Holy Scripture frequently sets it off. I'm not trying to imitate other preachers. When I was at the Yale Divinity School back in the mid-1950s, we all tried to imitate our homiletics professor. He was really good, but we were terrible. We weren't (yet) authentic. Now that I'm in my 80s, I'd like to think I am. In any case, what you get is me.

I want to thank all the people of the churches these sermons were preached in. They listened and responded, sometimes laughed and even clapped. A preacher needs encouragement; otherwise, he just wants to take his manuscript and go home. Good Lord, the people of St. Mary's, St. Thomas, St. Barnabas on the Desert and St. Michael's Cathedral have been wonderful.

The Rt. Rev. John S. Thornton
Boise, Idaho
June 2014

# As regarding this new edition...

Since the third printing of *The Backside of God* sold out, a number of people have asked me if I'd planned to have more printed. It pleased me that they would ask; but, in fact, I hadn't planned to have more printed. I was busy with other things; and, of course, there was the cost.

However, my friends Stuart and Lisa Hotchkiss came along and incited my willingness, indeed my enthusiasm, to republish *The Backside of God*. In the process, we decided to lengthen the book by adding, first three, then four, then five new sermons – all preached at Episcopal churches in either Lebanon or Salem, Oregon – as well as another, a sixth, preached at the annual convention of the Episcopal Diocese of Idaho in 1991. Without Stuart and Lisa, I doubt that I would have done this. I'm grateful for the intervention into my lassitude.

I don't know how many times I've reread the sermons in the original book. They still interest me. It sounds prideful, I know, but they delight me. I've even had to wipe away a surreptitious tear while reading "The Creation Of The World." What surprises me, maybe most, is that so many people comment about "The Christ Child And The Farm Set."

Editing is full of amusements and horrors. No matter how many people read a manuscript or a publisher's proof, they will, inevitably, miss some glaring typo. You pray that a typo won't be so ridiculous that the reader will howl. This happened with the last book, *Good Seed and Zizania*. The blessing that I've used at baptisms and confirmations over the years has a doozy in it. Sorry. It says, "I bless your hips, that you may speak nothing but the Gospel of Jesus." Can you believe it? Hips. It's supposed to be "lips," the only logical word in the context. It's a good reminder of my imperfections — not to mention those of my fellow proofreaders. By the grace of print-on-demand technology, that typo has been fixed!

Finally, I want you to notice that I have dedicated this book to Jan's and my parents: Andrew Robertson Thornton, Getrude Mae (Nicol) Thornton, William DeBoer, and Dorothy Amelia (Muyskens) DeBoer. How lucky we were to have such parents. They gave us life and, in many ways, they still do. I pray everyone such grace.

The Rt. Rev. John S. Thornton
Taucross Farm
Scio, Oregon
September 2016

# The Backside Of God

My wife, Jan, and I were in the Starbucks by the Fred Meyer store in Albany, Oregon. (Our small farm is about 20 miles away.) It was a hot afternoon; so we stopped in for some cool mocha Frappaccinos® and *The New York Times*. We sat down at a little round table by the window and were getting our infusion of Frappaccino® and poring over the paper, Jan reading the editorials and I the columnists (David Brooks, Paul Krugman, Thomas Friedman, Gail Collins, et al.) when this young man pulled up a chair, sat down and said, "May I give you a blessing and pray with you?" Give us a blessing? Pray with us? Here? In Starbucks? Right now? "NO!" rose up from deep recesses in my psyche, but I didn't let it out of my mouth. This may sound conceited and prideful and arrogant, but I don't think we looked like the worst sinners in that place. However, I told myself, as I tell others to say to themselves, "This is my son, my beloved, with whom I am well pleased," not trying to be God, but godly. Maybe he thought he'd be safe with us, and he was right. He was. The young man had scrubbed himself antiseptic and shiny. He had glued his blond hair up into little spikes on top of his head. His overalls reeked of OxiClean. He had studs or rhinestones – I can't remember which – in his ears and on the left side of his nose. There was nothing objectionable about him. Only a little brash, as the innocent can be. To avoid the blessing/praying scene, I said, "Tell us about you." And he did. He was a member of the Vineyard Christian Fellowship down the road. He loved the Lord Jesus. He was at peace with God and the whole world. His calling was to go around blessing and praying with people. He intended to go to a Bible school in

California. That's when Jan, ever the schoolteacher, gave him a brief, though earnest, lecture about going to a college or university. The Lord would give him mobs of pagans to bless and pray for there, I thought. He seemed as resistant to that idea as I was to receiving his blessing and praying with him there in Starbucks. To bring it all to a nice conclusion, I said, "You know, we could join hands and close our eyes and say familiar words; but you, by coming to our table and speaking with us, have given us a very special blessing. Thank you." With that, he got up and left, feeling, I hope, triumphant. He had taken a risk and made a connection with two old folks and increased the possibility of the world's peace. It was a way of caring that both Jan and I were, well, inspired by. As he went out the door, I said, "Jan, look...look at him. That's the backside of God."

Oh, I'd like to tell you about "the backside of God."

In the 33rd chapter of Exodus, "Mother" Moses and his "babies" – that's what Moses called the Hebrew tribes, he was so sick of their whimpering and whining – were out there in the "wilderness," which was about as lush as Nevada. Moses screamed at the heavens. Did I conceive these people? Did I give birth to these people? Do you expect me to be their nursemaid? Go ahead and kill me. See if I care. The Hebrew tribes weren't slaves anymore, but, oh, they had a hankering to go back to Egypt, even back to slavery if it meant three square meals a day. In Egypt, they had "fish and cucumbers and melons and leeks and onions and garlic." Garlic?! (My version of the Garden of Eden story is that God said to Adam and Eve, "Eat all the fruits and vegetables you want; just don't eat the garlic." Of course, that's the first thing they did. They pulled it up and ate it raw. To deny the guilt of their disobedience, they tried to convince each other that it tasted good and was really good for you. It has been the curse of cuisine ever since. That's what my Bible says.) That hand-to-mouth existence under Moses' leadership was getting old. They were angry and rebellious and, as it says in Exodus 32, so deranged that they started killing each other. All they had to eat was manna, gooey manna, breakfast, lunch and dinner. A couple of wags tried to find the humor in the situation and wrote a little song:

> Manna in the morning,
> Manna in the evening,
> Manna at suppertime;
> All we get is manna;
> It's manna all the time.

That's not in the Bible. I'm making that up, just to keep you awake.

The Lord, who had picked them to be a "chosen" people, had had enough of them. That's where Chapter 33 begins. Moses and the Lord are having words with each other. The Lord says to Moses, "You can just take these people and go to – Canaan. Let me tell you, it may be heaven compared to this hell, even if you have to live among the Canaanites...and the Amorites...and the Hittites...and Perizzites...and the Hivites...and the Jebusites...and a lot of other nasty and hateful and murderous people. Good luck, because I'm not going with you. If I did, I'd see to it that you were wiped out along the way. You're a bunch of jerks." ("Jerks" is a loose translation of the Hebrew, which in cleaned-up Bibles, usually reads "stiff-necked people." Same thing.) When the tribes got wind of that kiss-off, they got religious and all dolled up and danced around, to placate the Lord. The Lord was not impressed. But Moses wouldn't give up on behalf

3

of his "babies." He'd go into "the tent of meeting" for some dialogue with the Lord. "Thus the Lord used to speak with Moses face to face, as one speaks to a friend," it says. The "face to face" thing is a contradiction, because the Lord's face is the one thing Moses – or anybody else – will never see. And now it's time to get into that.

Oh, I love Chapter 33 of Exodus. It's mythologized history, of course. And the anthropomorphisms are charming. The Lord has a face and a hand and speaks perfect Hebrew. But none of that makes it untrue. It is true – and absolutely true – of the Hebrew's experience of the Holy One during the time they were wandering around the desert. What comes next is something every God-thinking person should take to heart. It's essential to the sanity and stability of every psyche and every society. It puts human beings and nations in their place. Here's how the authors of Exodus tell it. Moses and the Lord are having this dialogue. The Lord says, "Moses, I know everything about you." And Moses says, "Lord, I'd like to know everything about you, too." "Oh no, you wouldn't," says the Lord. "If you ever saw my face, you'd die. Here's the best I can do for you, Moses. You climb up on that rock over there, and I'll cover your eyes with my hand and walk past; then I'll take my hand away, and all you'll ever see of me is my backside as I go off into the distance."

Now this is one of the most important concepts in Judaic and Christian theology. It's called, yes, "the backside of God." We'll never see God's face, but we'll frequently, continually see God's backside. Though we'll never know God fully (in this life), we will know God partially. God is incomprehensible. St. Athanasius is my authority: "The Father is incomprehensible, the Son is incomprehensible, and the Holy Ghost is incomprehensible." I've always been suspicious of people who claim to comprehend more about God than can be comprehended.

We're smart to speak, with reverence, of "the mystery of God." I zone out when I hear people's huffy certitudes about the uncreated, unconditioned One. However, there are some things in my experience in life and my reflections on Scripture that persuade me are a good look at the backside of God. Caring, simple caring, is one of them. It's through lowliness that the Most High God is revealed so convincingly.

We preachers often leave the impression that, apart from hyper-religiosity and philanthropy, even a kind of martyrdom, there's not much hope for salvation. The Jesus I comprehend would take a much softer approach. Since our days in Sunday school, a big part of our identity as Christians has been Matthew 25: "I was hungry, and you gave me something to eat; I was thirsty, and you gave me something to drink; I was a stranger, and you welcomed me; I had no clothes, and you gave me something to wear; I was sick, and you cared for me; I was in prison, and you came to see me." You can be sure that, when those who do those things leave, others see the backside of God. It was Mother Teresa of Calcutta who said, wise to our limitations, "(Just) do little things with great love." There's not a person in this church who doesn't. You don't call attention to it. You quickly forget all about it. You go on to the next opportunity to care. And if I called you "saints," you'd get all embarrassed and deny it. We're just ordinary folks, you'd say.

There's a stanza in The Reverend Eli Jenkins evening prayer in Dylan Thomas's *Under Milk Wood:*

"We are not wholly bad or good
Who live our lives under Milk Wood.
And thou, I know, will be the first,
To see our best side, not our worst."

+John S. Thornton

"Our best side," our caring side, my loves, is the backside of God.

The Rt. Rev. John S. Thornton
St. Thomas Church
Ketchum, Idaho
August 4, 2013

# Take Time For Paradise

This is the first in a series of sermons on our Eucharistic liturgy. My task is to talk about the whole purpose of the liturgy. There will be others, on the Peace, the Offertory, the Fraction, and the Dismissal. As for the purpose of our liturgy, I'll take a roundabout way; but we'll get there. Bear with me.

I've read quite a few books on liturgy. In my opinion, the best book on liturgy isn't on liturgy at all. It's on baseball. The book is A. Bartlett ("Bart") Giamatti's *Take Time for Paradise*.

I have a history with *Take Time for Paradise*.

Sometime back in the mid-1990s, I got a call from a chaplain at the Mountain Home Air Force Base in Idaho. He asked me if I would give the benediction at their National Prayer Day Breakfast. I said, "Sure, I'd be happy to." Then he told me that the speaker would be Tommy Lasorda, the Manager of the Los Angeles Dodgers. (He was also featured in those SlimFast® ads.) "Wow," I said, "I'd love to hear Tommy Lasorda speak." I got the impression that it was a sure thing. However, the chaplain added a little caveat, with a voice so smooth that it screamed uncertainty. "If for some reason 'Tommy' – as if the two of them were on a first-name basis – couldn't make it, would you be the speaker?" Three months away from an event, you agree to almost anything. I did. Within minutes, I was in a panic about what I had agreed to. The chaplain promised to stay in touch. The days of unease went by.

A week before the National Prayer Day Breakfast, I called the chaplain. "Is Tommy Lasorda coming?" "He plans to, though he's having a little trouble arranging transportation." I accepted that as a "yes." On Monday before the National Prayer Day Breakfast, I called the chaplain again. "Is Tommy Lasorda still planning to be there?" "He says so, but he still hasn't worked out the transportation." What? Is it really that hard to get from Los Angeles to Mountain Home? On the Wednesday before the National Prayer Day Breakfast, I called the chaplain again. "Is Tommy Lasorda going to make it?" "He'd like to, but he wants us to send an F-16 to pick him up. We can't do that. It looks like you're going to be the speaker." Oh, God.

I could just see it. An officers' club jam-packed with Air Force personnel and their spouses and their children, every one of them excited about seeing and hearing the legendary Tommy Lasorda. And what do they get? The Episcopal Bishop of Idaho. A preacher.

It was now the Thursday before the National Prayer Day Breakfast. Jan and I were in Buhl at the time, working with the church there. We got into our car and drove as fast as the law allowed – maybe a little faster – to the Barnes & Noble in Twin Falls. I needed some books on baseball, in an attempt not to disappoint people too much.

Barnes & Noble did have some books on baseball, mostly big picture books. I needed little word books. We picked two of them, David Halberstam's *The Summer of '49* and A. Bartlett ("Bart") Giamatti's *Take Time for Paradise*. Back to Buhl we went, Jan driving, I scanning the two books. *The Summer of '49* was too fat; so I put it aside. *Take Time for Paradise* was a lot skinnier; so I started to read it cover to cover. It was so beautifully written that I didn't notice how fast — or slow — Jan was driving.

Bart Giamatti was the Commissioner of Baseball from April 1, 1989 until September 1, 1989. He died of a heart attack after only five months in office. He had been the President of Yale University, but he resigned to take the job he had always wanted. He loved baseball and he understood its philosophy, its geometry, its numerology, its strategy and tactics *and* its rites and ceremonies. He made baseball's hunger for homecoming as important as Homer's *The Odyssey*.

By bedtime on Thursday, I had a speech, written on the back of seven envelopes. It was either going to work or be a colossal flop and the whole Episcopal Church in the United States of America would be humiliated. We slept well, but not long. By five in the morning, we were up, showered, dressed and on our way from Buhl to the Mountain Home Air Force Base.

We got to the gate of the Base at about 07:30. I pulled into the guardhouse parking lot and hurried in. An MP noticed my collar and asked, "Are you here for the National Prayer Day Breakfast?" "I am," I said. "Follow me, sir!" Who was I to disobey orders? He ran to his patrol car, got in, started the engine, turned on the flashing lights and careened out of the parking lot. We followed right behind him. We'd never had that kind of treatment before. We felt like the President and the First Lady. When we got to the officers' club, the MP skidded to a stop, jumped out and shouted, "Park here, sir!" It made no difference to him that it said "No Parking." He was making lawbreaking so much fun.

There were a lot of people milling around in the entrance of the officers' club, but the chaplain elbowed his way through and greeted us. I said, "Could you take me to a private room so that I can look over my speech? Let me know when it's time for breakfast." No problem. I looked over what I had written on the backs of the envelopes, scratched off some lines, scribbled some new ones. I was getting confident and panicky at the same time. Then the chaplain came and told me that it was time for breakfast. Jan and I were seated at the head table, on the dais. I sat on the chair that Tommy Lasorda was supposed to have sat on, and I felt people's excitement dying down. No Tommy Lasorda. A guy with his collar on backwards. And we paid for this. We ate.

I was introduced by the chaplain. There was polite applause. I said, "In case you haven't noticed, I'm not Tommy Lasorda." They roared. To them, that was funny. I thought, I think I'm going to like this audience. "You've come to hear Tommy Lasorda talk about baseball; so I'm going to talk about baseball. Well, you say, you don't know anything about baseball. What difference does that make?" I said. "People talk about things they don't know anything about all the time. If Tommy Lasorda were here and talked about Process Theology, you'd love it." They roared. I was having fun. They were egging me on.

First, I talked about Jackie Robinson and baseball as meritocracy. It's not whom you know, it's what you can do that matters. You could see "yes" on every face. The audience was full of scrambled eggs and sausage patties and hash browns and alleluias.

Then I talked about baseball as a parable. Baseball is America's parable. It's a universal parable. It's about coming home again and having a reunion with those who care most about you. It's like the ancient myth of Odysseus, who risked whatever he had to risk and suffered whatever he had to suffer to get home again.

And on and on. When it was all over, I signed Tommy Lasorda baseball cards with my own name. One woman came up and told me, "Whenever I see those SlimFast® ads, I'll think of you." I've rarely had so much fun.

In baseball, there are four bases, but the fourth base isn't called "fourth base." It's called "home." The object of baseball is to get on base and around the bases and back home again. But once you get a hit or a walk – with the exception of a "home run," for which you get safe passage around all the bases – you're out there all alone in a dangerous world. Everybody out there is out there to make sure you'll never get home again. They can make it "swift and savage." If you take too long a lead off first, the pitcher can pick you off. If you try to steal second, the catcher can throw you out. If you take too big a lead off second and head for third, you can get trapped between the second and third basemen and get tagged out ingloriously. If a fielder has the "arm," he can throw you out at second or third or home. Everybody out there is practiced and primed to make you fail. But when you do get home again, there's a combustion of glee and a compaction of boyish physicality, high-fiving and back-slapping and hugs. The "family" is together again!

Even if you don't play baseball or never have, that's your story. The world isn't always a safe place. It can be dangerous and often is. But the mature and healthy person doesn't slink from it, loves the challenges, takes the risks, wins some, loses some. Nonetheless, we all get weary and need to go home again. "Ye, who are weary, come home."

All the elements of our Eucharistic liturgy combine to make our worship an experience of coming home again. Here there is the sense of safety and security. Here there is "the freedom from wariness." Here there is the coloration and "aroma of inclusiveness." Here there is the atmosphere of absolution and embracement. Here there is the affirmation of individuality and autonomy. Here there is the celebration of the giftedness and goodness of each person. Here there is the pulsating and palpable presence of the mystical Christ. Here is "home," a state of belonging to all whose hearts are in the heart of Christ. That's where we are, home again, as we kneel and eat the sacred bread and drink the sacred wine. That's how we "take time for paradise."

The Rt. Rev. John S. Thornton
St. Michael's Cathedral
Boise, Idaho
March 9, 2014

# The Creation Of The World

"What paralyzes life is a lack of faith and
a lack of audacity."

PIERRE TEILHARD DE CHARDIN

—✺—

I was working on a sermon about the Book of Daniel. Daniel, you know, right after Ezekiel and right before Hosea. You've read it. You have read it, haven't you? What? Not since you took a Bible as Literature class in college! It's one of the greatest allegories in the history of literature and merits many re-readings. There's the story about Daniel, the Jewish Daniel, getting heaved into a lions' den, to be mauled and masticated by the beasts. However, the Lord God causes the lions to have lockjaw. When the king's cronies look in the next day, expecting to see nothing but a finger, maybe, or an ear, there's Daniel all snuggled up with the lions as if they were pussycats. And there's the story about Shadrach, Meshach and Abednego, all Jews, being shoved into a "fiery furnace," superheated to seven times its hitherto hottest. When the king's cronies open up the furnace a couple of days later, thinking there'd be nothing left of them but blackened tibia, there they are, as if they'd just come back from a vacation in Bermuda. And there's the story about King Nebuchadnezzar's bad dream about a huge statue with the head made of gold and the chest and arms made of silver and the torso and thighs made of bronze and the legs made of iron and the feet, oh, oh, the feet made of clay. Stomp on the feet and the whole things falls over and shatters into a million pieces. Daniel, though it purports to be about ancient history, is, in fact, about the current situation in Palestine in about 175 B.C., when the Jews were oppressed and persecuted under Antiochus Epiphanes. "Epiphanes" is the name he gave himself. It's Greek for "illustrious." Antiochus the Illustrious he was, in his own estimation. The Jews, however, called him "Antiochus Epimanes." "Epimanes" is Greek for "nincompoop" and a lot worse things, which can't be uttered in church.

However, I decided not to do that sermon; so you'll have to wait, not that you can't. Something else urged itself into my heart, and it has been on my tongue since last Monday. It came to me directly from the Holy God via *The Idaho Statesman*. Really. It came as a totally unexpected gift.

You may remember my sermon about baseball, "Take Time for Paradise." This is another sermon about baseball.

*The New York Times*, which I read routinely, has good writers, but it doesn't have all of them. *The Idaho Statesman* has some too, including one named Trevor Phibbs. He wrote a story, published in the Monday, April 28th edition, about Eddie Gordon, nicknamed "Fast Eddie." Fast Eddie was born with Down syndrome. He's a senior at Timberline High School in Boise. He's on the baseball team, the "Wolves." He's the batboy, the cheerleader, the enforcer of morale. He's there to give everybody lessons in humanity, and they're learning things that will last a lifetime.

In appreciation for Eddie Gordon's contributions to the baseball program (and to the whole school for that matter), the Timberline coach worked it out with the Centennial (High School) coach to make it a moment of glory for Eddie. Eddie would be the leadoff batter. He had never been a batter.

I read the story with wet eyes.

I said to Jan, "Do you know where we're going this evening?"

"No, where?"

"We're going to the Timberline-Centennial baseball game. I have to see it. I have to be present for the creation of the world."

"You have to be present for the creation of the world? What are you talking about?"

I'll tell you all what I was talking about. The world is always either being created or being destroyed. You may think that's overstating the case, but it's ancient Jewish wisdom. I take it seriously. Say some people are creators and some are destroyers or, at least, let the destroyers get the upper hand. If we're going to have a world, the creators have to work harder and faster and longer than the destroyers. I want to be a creator and I want to be around creators. I was pretty sure I'd be around them on Monday night, and I was right.

Fast Eddie's life has obviously been graced by great parenting. His mom, Becky, told the reporter, "We didn't know any different. We never got hung up on the fact that he has Down syndrome. He was our son and we love him." Love such as that is the impulse of all creation. Eddie's mom sounds like God in the story of Jesus' baptism: "This is my son, my beloved, with whom I am well pleased." That means well-pleased; and if every once in a while not so well pleasing, still and forever well-pleased. No wonder Eddie is such an extraordinary human being and inspires others to reach, reach, reach for their extraordinariness. The catcher, a senior, summed it up: "Whenever he comes through the gate, he always has this huge smile on his face. We see him and we're, like, 'Man, it must be a good day.'"

It doesn't take an old preacher to make the case. The shortstop, who's only a sophomore – what does that make him, fifteen? – said, "He's pretty much my biggest inspiration. He's made me a better person. I look at life in a whole different way. Life doesn't revolve around baseball. It revolves around being a good person." Fifteen years old! That's one of the most spiritually mature things I've ever read or heard. (Shortstopping, by the way, is a special vocation, limited to the fleet-footed and quick-witted. Bart Giamatti, in his book, *Take Time for Paradise*, says, "There are no dragons in baseball, only shortstops.")

I've never met the Timberline baseball coach, Larry Price. I'd never heard of Coach Price before last Monday morning, when I read the paper. I suppose he's a teacher at Timberline as well as a coach. In my parlance, he's also a priest. I don't mean that he's ordained in some church. I mean that he's a priest in the truest sense. A priest is someone, man, woman, boy, girl, who knows that he/she stands between human beings and God and introduces one to the Other, so that a mutual love affair can begin and, we hope and pray, end in "the divine union." That describes Coach Price. Somehow, he has introduced teenagers to things that are holy, deep within themselves, and has given those young people permission to act on them. They can see that his life is not "paralyzed by a lack of faith and a lack of audacity."

All of that gives me a chance to remind you that we're not a congregation with a priest or two (and one old bishop). We're, by Baptism, a priesthood; and when we gather to make Eucharist, one or two of us step forward to preside on behalf of us all. Then we all leave to be priests in the midst of the world, making every place an altar and every thing a sacrament. Take a lesson from the coach.

On Monday evening, at six o'clock, there was a Senior Night ceremony. Moms and dads accompanied their sons to the home plate to be honored. It took a while, but it was touching. If your mind works the way mine does, you would have seen little holy trinities standing there, mom, dad, son, one after another. Then the game started.

Fast Eddie, with the coach nearly embracing him, stepped up to the plate. The Centennial pitcher moved halfway between the mound and the home plate. Underhanded, he lobbed the ball. Fast Eddie swung – and missed. Strike One. The crowd groaned. The pitcher tossed another one. Fast Eddie swung – and missed. Strike Two. The crowd was in agony. The coach adjusted Fast Eddie's hands on the bat. One more pitch arched its way toward destiny. Fast Eddie swung. He tipped it! Technically, it was a foul ball, but Fast Eddie took off for first base. The crowd went nuts: "Go! Go! Go!" And Fast Eddie went. The catcher ran after the ball, picked it up and, deliberately, threw it over the first baseman's head into right field. Fast Eddie was on his way to second. "Go! Go! Go!" The first baseman finally got the ball and, deliberately, threw it over the heads of the shortstop and the third baseman into left field. Fast Eddie was on his way to third. "Go! Go! Go!" By the time the left fielder picked up the ball, Fast Eddie was on his way to home base. I don't know if he slid into it or just jumped up and down on it. He was home, the destination of baseball, the destination of the human heart. The Wolves galloped out of the dugout and piled on him and picked him up off the ground and put him up on their shoulders and carried him back to the dugout, he waving his arms in triumph, while the crowd was screaming, it seemed to me, "Holy, holy, holy, Lord God of hosts, heaven and earth are full of your glory." It was just as I thought. We were present for the creation of the world. It was audacious, with the audacity of plain and pure goodness.

Whenever we raise each other up, we're raising ourselves up, too; and our hearts converge in the heart of the Holy One. The possibility always exists, on the baseball field, in the classroom, at home, in offices and shops, in our churches and synagogues and mosques and temples and wards. Whenever that possibility becomes a reality, the Creator of heaven and earth thunders, "Behold, it is very good."

The Rt. Rev. John S. Thornton
St. Michael's Cathedral
Boise, Idaho
May 4, 2014

# Baptism: Mine

On June 19, 1933, nine months and two weeks after I was born, my parents had me made a Christian. I'm sure they didn't sit down at the kitchen table one night and say, "We've got to do something about this kid or he'll grow up to make trouble for the world." I have a photograph of myself as a toddler. I didn't look dangerous. But looks can deceive. As toddlers, even the Mafiosi look like cherubs. My parents just did what most parents did back in those days: they had me baptized. They scrubbed me down and dressed me up and took me bodily to the Union Congregational Church in Somonauk, Illinois. (We lived in that little town.) I had nothing to say about it. I was hardly more than an object, though of affection, I'm sure. I had a will, and probably a very strong one, judging by my current condition; but it had to do mostly with getting fed and getting changed and getting sleep. Once those things were taken care of, I suppose I didn't much care what they did. I have no memory of the baptism.

Since it was in a Congregational church, I know I wasn't "dunked," as they say, bare naked in a huge bowl of warm water. I doubt that the minister even poured water over my head, three times, once for the Father, once for the Son and once for the Holy Spirit. Chances are, I was kind of splashed or sprinkled and quickly mopped up and prayed over. It was the Protestant way. Not too much fuss. I don't know if I winced dumbly or, in shock, wailed or just kind of passed out. It couldn't have been a big scene. My baptism was never the topic of conversation in our household, not from that day to this. Anyway, I became a Christian in a splash or a sprinkle and with some words, not that I was aware of it. My parents promised, vowed, and swore that I'd keep my covenant with Christ. It was high hope, because they really had no idea how I would turn out.

Why do people do this with infants? I mean scrub them down and dress them up and take them bodily to the church for Baptism? Why did my parents do that with me? I know they didn't believe in magic. It was 1933. It was the Great Depression. Along with everybody else in town, they were dealing with harsh realities, dollar by dollar. And I know that they didn't believe that, if I wasn't baptized and died, I wouldn't "go to heaven." That was one of the looniest ideas around back in those days. They were, after all, Protestants, skeptics, dissenters and would have sensed the wrongness of that and raged more than laughed about it. A loving God not loving unbaptized babies? Phooey! (Today, I can hardly believe how much ignorance and superstition and outright cruelty passes for the Christian religion.) And it wasn't because my parents had some well thought-out theology of Baptism, such as "the sacrament of prevenient grace," for which you just about have to go to seminary. I'll bet they never heard of it. I think they had me baptized for the simplest of reasons: they were grateful for their child and proud of him and, I have no doubt, knew that not everything in their lives was the direct result of their own efforts. Some things were, well, just a gift. "Grace" it's called. Baptism was one way, maybe the best way, to express it. It was as if they were repeating God's line in the story of Jesus' baptism: "This is my son, my beloved, with whom I am pleased." Then they had cake.

The fact is that, without one thought about God or Jesus Christ or the Holy Spirit or sin or grace or anything beyond my immediate needs, I was made a Christian, equal, as we Protestants used to say, to "the Pope in Rome." On the conscious level, it meant nothing to me. But heaven only knows what goes on in the unconscious. Had any of "the seven-fold gifts of the Spirit" been conferred on me by that rite? (The seven-fold gifts of the Spirit by the way, from the description of the Messiah in the eleventh chapter of Isaiah, are wisdom, understanding, counsel, fortitude, knowledge, piety and the fear of the Lord. I have the last one in spades, if by "fear" we mean "awe;" but I'm short, as you must realize, on piety. "Piety," however, wasn't in the original Hebrew text. It was added in the Latin Vulgate; so I don't feel all that bad about it.) Only time will tell how many of the gifts, if any, I was given. I'm waiting. Maybe you are, too.

In Somonauk and in Cambridge City, Indiana, where we moved when I was two, and Bluffton, Indiana, where we moved when I was five, our parents took us (my older brother and older sister and me) to Sunday school every Sunday. I should say that our mother took us. Our father drove and, as I recall, preferred to stay in the car and read the Sunday paper. However, I do remember his being inside once, in a pew, in a vise between our mother and some Methodist lady, for the Children's Day program in the church in Cambridge City. In the chancel, behind the pulpit, there was a long line of children, each holding some kind of gardening tool and each, one by one, reading a line off a slip of paper. I had a rake. When my turn came, I raised the rake as high as I could and muffed my line. My first theatrical performance was a flop. Our father was too gentle a man even to hint at anything but brilliance.

When I was seven, our father died of a coronary thrombosis. Our shocked and grieving and, I must say, impoverished family moved from Bluffton, Indiana to Elgin, Illinois, where both our father and mother had grown up. Though our lives were changed dramatically, there was never a time when our mother didn't take us to Sunday school at the First Congregational Church. We went obediently, though not against our wills. My fifth grade Sunday school teacher left no doubt in our minds that, if the Messiah were to come again, he'd play shortstop for the Chicago Cubs. There would be hell to pay for the other teams in the league. For the Cubs fans, it would be heaven on earth. We must have learned something about the Bible that year, but I can't remember what it was. In church, on Communion Sundays, they'd pass around silver plates with piles of three-quarter inch squares of Wonder Bread on them and round silver trays with tiny glass cups filled two-thirds to the top with grape juice, each cup in a hole in concentric circles of holes. We gulped the elements down without a fleeting thought about the Real Presence, about which we'd never heard anything anyway. Nonetheless, there was something good and kind of holy about it. We were nurtured and formed in that place, in the Protestant tradition, for which I remain deeply grateful, in spite of the things I think aren't right about it. I could go on and on with this autobiography, but I won't. You've heard enough.

In my case, did Baptism work? I should use the Church's language. Was it efficacious? I'm really not the judge of that. God is. However, you may have some opinions, which I suggest you keep to yourselves. I don't pretend to be a paragon of virtue or a model Christian. But I can tell you that, at age 76, I've never been more convinced and more convicted that Jesus of Nazareth was the Risen Human Being, risen from among the "dead," all those who don't or won't love, all the while running around as healthy as horses. My life's goal is to rise with him, to overcome my fear of loving, to love "carefreely." I have a long, long way to go. Consider me a devout evolutionist. When I consider what we're doing to each other all over the world today, I wonder if the "apes" would deny any connection with us. I can see them there, on their haunches, in a huddle in the tall savannah grass, complaining, "So those human beings think they're the crown of creation." If there's ever going to be peace and happiness on this planet, the whole human race has to evolve…and evolve…and evolve, until it has evolved into the likeness of Christ, the incarnation of the love of God. So why do I do this thing called "church" all the time? Not to be seen. (I'm happy to stay down on the farm with my chickens – and my chick.) Or to earn merits. After all, there was a Reformation. I do it because this is the place where, in Word and Sacrament and community, the Holy Spirit seems to have the best chance of softening my heart and strengthening my will to love the world and everything and everybody in it, as I believe Jesus did. And when I say "community," I mean you. I get my courage to love from you. I could name names actually. We get it from each other. And many of us got it from our parents, who scrubbed us down and dressed us up and took us bodily to a church to be baptized. All for love.

The Rt. Rev. John S. Thornton
St. Mary's Episcopal Church
Eugene, Oregon
January 25, 2009

# Jezebel

"So what's the advantage in getting everything the world has to offer but destroying your soul in the process?"

- LUKE 9:25

Summertime is a good time to retell some of those old Bible stories. Today's story is one of many about Elijah, the prophet.

In the passage which was read a few minutes ago, Elijah is out of the country, clear down to Mount Horeb. His life isn't worth a plug shekel. Jezebel, King Ahab's wife, has a contract out on him. Let me tell you why.

There was a drought and famine in Israel. Not a drop of rain. Not a drop of dew. The land couldn't produce a weed. Fish flopped around in the receding puddles in what once were rivers. People were dying. It was bad. Elijah was convinced that the drought and the famine and the death of Israelites was the direct result of Ahab's and Jezebel's actions. Particularly Jezebel's. She had ordered the slaying of the prophets of the Lord, the God of Israel, and wouldn't be happy until all of them were dead and underground. So Elijah, the prophet of the Lord, got up his courage to confront Ahab. "You and that wife of yours have brought on this disaster by your worship of Baal, that good-for-nothing, two-shekel god." Then Elijah proposed a contest to prove that Baal had no power whatsoever, but that the Lord, the God of Israel, had it all. Here's how it worked.

They killed two bulls, one for the prophets of Baal and one for Elijah. They butchered them. The prophets of Baal put the pieces of their bull on a heap of dry wood, for a triumphant barbeque. All they needed was fire from heaven. O Baal, send down fire from heaven. Now! Baal!! Please!!! Nothing. Not a spark. Not a puff of smoke. Nothing. Only embarrassment and humiliation and shameful defeat. Then it was Elijah's turn. He took twelve stones, one for each of the twelve tribes of Israel, and built an altar. He stacked wood on the altar and laid the pieces of his bull on the wood. Showman that he was, he had his servant pour water all over everything, once, twice, three times. And Elijah dug a trench around the altar and filled it with water. There wasn't anything flammable on or around or anywhere near the altar. O, Lord, the God of Abraham and Isaac and Jacob, show these people that you and only you are the Lord. And, whoosh, fire fell from heaven and consumed the meat...and the wood...and the twelve stones...and the dust all around...and everything. There was nothing left but a big black spot where everything had been. The spectators fell down on their knees and bowed and bowed and bowed for dear life. At Elijah's command, his people grabbed all the prophets of Baal, took them down to the Wadi Kishon and merrily slew them. Four hundred and fifty of them. How's that for evangelism? Don't worry, it's mythologized history, likely more mythology than history.

We do know that Ahab and Jezebel were not happy with Elijah. Jezebel especially was determined to get even, for which reason Elijah left the country and was in hiding. However, for the love of

Israel and the love of the Lord, the God of Israel, he just couldn't stay away. What happened next brought out every bit of his wrath, as a stand-in for the Lord.

It had to do with a vineyard near the palace. It belonged to a man named Naboth, and it had been in his family for generations. They had flung or lugged every stone off that land and built a wall. They had planted and watered every vine. They had tugged out every weed. Year after year, they had expertly pruned the vines. They loved that place. But Ahab would love to have it, so that his servants could plant a beautiful vegetable garden for him. Cucumbers... eggplants...leeks...garlic. Garlic?! (Ahab ate a lot of garlic. With his breath, he could ward off Jezebel and all his servants and all his subjects and the Devil and germs at the same time. The Bible doesn't say anything like that. I just want to make sure that you don't forget what my opinion of garlic is.) Ahab, crown in hand, went to Naboth and made him an offer. It was, by Ahab's standards, more than fair. He'd pay Naboth whatever he thought the vineyard was worth – or more if he wanted. Or he'd buy him a vineyard somewhere else, anywhere else, no matter what the cost. Just tell him where. No deal. Naboth was polite about it, but he wanted the king to understand that he wouldn't dig up the vines and the bones of his ancestors for any amount of money. Ahab, King of Israel, sulking, went back to the palace and straight to bed. He pulled the covers over his head so that his world would be as small and as dark as a grave. He couldn't live in a world in which his wealth was useless...in which his power was useless...in which his sorry, sorry self was utterly useless. (In case you've lost some confidence in my biblical interpretation, I want you to know that I'm not making this up. In so many words, the Bible says exactly that.)

Into the bedroom came Jezebel, to find the king in bed, with the covers over his head. She yanked those covers off and yelled, "What, in Baal's name, are you doing?" So he told her what had happened at Naboth's vineyard. "Snap out of it, you wimp! Get up! Get something to eat! Act like a king! And leave the vineyard to me."

You need to know a little about Jezebel. Her dad was the King of Tyre. All she knew was wealth and power. Her behavior, as my social worker friends would say, was the result of bad parenting. Her dad and mom were too busy kinging and queening to do what's necessary to form the character of a decent human being. Nobody ever said "No" to little Jezebel. Early in childhood, she learned that, with tantrums, she could be omnipotent, even among potentates. It became the pattern of her life. Her behavior as an adult wasn't much different from her behavior as a child. Then this adult/child was married off to the King of Israel. (By the way, this is a perfectly logical deduction. However, for my entire analysis, I didn't quote the Bible once.)

Leave the vineyard to me, she said. So she wrote a letter to all the important people in the city and asked them, on a my-wish-is-my-command basis, to put on a banquet in honor of that fine citizen Naboth. Have him sit in the middle of the head table. Have two "scoundrels" (that's the word used in the Bible, though, in fact, they were hired killers) sit on either side of him. Once everybody is practically brainless from all the wine, have those two guys get up and proclaim that Naboth has cursed both the king and Baal. And that's exactly what they did. And, of course, everybody believed them. Nobody was sober enough to ask, "When did he do that?" or "How did he do that" or "How do you know that he did that?"

Or if there were any libertarians present, "So what?" The lovers of truth are few and always have been. In their half-drunken fury, they took the so-called blasphemer outside the city walls and stoned him to death. It was so satisfying to rid the city of an unrighteous man. Then they staggered home and slept it off. Jezebel, when she was given the news, waltzed into Ahab's bedroom and said, "Guess what, Abby (she never called him "highness;" she always called him Abby), Naboth died, poor fellow. Now you can get that vineyard." How Jezebel pulled that off was an open secret. Everybody pretended not to know that she was behind it. Ahab suspected; but of course, he was spineless.

When Elijah got wind of it, he was mad. He was outraged. He was furious with a fury that would not diminish. At the risk of his life, he went straight to Ahab, breathing "the word of the Lord." "You're just as guilty as your wife! Where the dogs licked up Naboth's blood they'll lick up Jezebel's – and yours, too!" Ahab had the honesty to repent (sackcloth, ashes, all that) and was spared. Not superego-less Jezebel. Later in the story, three eunuchs heave her out of a third story window, and she ends up in a heap of gore. By the time the dogs are through with her, there was nothing left of her but her skull and her feet and the palms of her hands. That's in the Bible.

I'm not going to say one word about such things as the divine wrath and the divine justice and the divine retribution. I can't make my mind go there. I would never, never attribute to God what we human beings do to each other and to ourselves in spite of God, the God of non-violence, the God of mercy, the God of compassion, the God of forgiveness, the God of love "that will not let us go." But I do remind myself – and now you – that the consequences of greed are awful. Those Medieval theologians knew what they were talking about when they called greed one of the "deadly" sins. It's both good theology and depth psychology. It's an observable, verifiable, universal fact. After we've destroyed the lives of other people, we finally destroy our own. Disrespected, unloved, miserable. And, with greed out of control, we can destroy whole economies as well. You do remember sub-prime mortgages and mortgage-backed securities and insurance swaps and "the housing bubble" and The Great Recession, don't you?

You'll be glad you came to church this morning because I'm going to tell you how to get rich, richer than Ahab and Jezebel ever dreamed that they or anybody else could ever be. You may want to take notes. Here's how. Imagine – believe – understand – and live as though you are the bread of life for the world and give yourself away. Then you'll be rich from all the reciprocities of love; rich even from the love that isn't reciprocated; rich from the satisfactions of simple service among those about whom you'd never make any judgments, considering your own imperfections; rich from friendships among people of every race, every color, every creed, every gender, everyone made in the image of God and each the bearer of God's grace. You'll be rich, oh so rich, from the joy that the world, with its calculus of wealth, can never give you and never take away.

So what's the advantage in getting everything the world has to offer but destroying your soul in the process?

The Rt. Rev. John S. Thornton
St. Michael's Cathedral
Boise, Idaho
August 12, 2012

# This Is Thou — But Thou Art Not This

Once your heart trains your eyes, you can see the Risen Christ everywhere.

Let me tell you some stories.

First story.

For the month of December and the month before Easter every year, I'm the Bishop-in-Residence at St. Barnabas on the Desert in Scottsdale, Arizona. I preach a couple of times each month, and I lecture almost every Wednesday evening. Jan and I stay in a parishioner's guesthouse. While there, I often go walking in the morning, up Hayden Road to McCormick Parkway, then over to Scottsdale Road, then down to Indian Bend Road, then home again. Starbucks is at the corner of Scottsdale Road and Indian Bend Road. I usually stop there to get a cup of coffee and *The New York Times*. A few months ago, I was all set to go on my walk; and, since I knew that I'd stop at Starbucks, I took my billfold off the chest of drawers, to take a few ones out of it. But there weren't any ones – or fives – or even tens. All I had was a twenty-dollar bill. So I stuffed that in my pocket and started out. When I got to the corner of McCormick Parkway and Scottsdale Road, I could see a gray shape – or shapes – against the grayness of the morning, about a sixteenth of a mile away. I was both curious and kind of fearful. When I was about fifty yards away, I could see that the shapes were a man and a shopping cart. The man was dressed in the gray and black clothes he must have found in a thrift shop somewhere. In the shopping cart were, I assumed, all his worldly possessions. I just knew he was going to ask me for money. And I wasn't going to lie to him and say, "Oh, gosh, I wish I could; but I don't have a cent on me this morning." This fifteen-second encounter with a total stranger was going to cost me twenty bucks! I went through paroxysms of stinginess and self-pity. Then we were only a few yards away from each other. Then we were side by side, just he and I among all the millions of people in this world. Side by side we were, he and I, on a narrow sidewalk. But he didn't ask me for money! He didn't say a word to me. He didn't even glance at me. He went right on pushing that cart, wheels rattling at every crack in the concrete. I was both relieved and somewhat disappointed, because his asking me for money might have been the divine imperative to give away everything I had at the moment. I turned and watched him go down Scottsdale Road, becoming once again a gray shape against the grayness of the morning. Suddenly, I realized who it was. It was Jesus, homeless still.

Second story.

St. Barnabas on the Desert belongs to something called the Interfaith Hospitality Network, which is an organization of Christian churches and Jewish temples that provides housing and meals for homeless families fifty-two weeks a year. St. Barnabas does it four times a year, a week each time. Parishioners do their very best to make the Sunday school rooms look like the Hilton Hotel. The meals are worthy of the dinner parties they have in their homes. The rule is that these families should be treated like the Holy Family. The last time they did this, just before Christmas, Jan and I spent the evening with the families. We slept in the library overnight. There were ten guests, four single moms, two black, two white, and six kids, two black, four white. The youngest was only a month old. This tiny black baby would have fit in a shoebox. She was all wrapped up in a blanket. I felt so sorry for her. She had a runny nose and, probably, infected ears. The moms, black and white, took turns holding her and cuddling her and rocking her and talking baby talk to her and singing. One sang,

"Away in a manger,
no crib for his bed,
the little Lord Jesus,
lay down his sweet head…"

It was then I realized who that baby was. She was the Christ Child.

Third story.

On the recommendation of discerning friends, Jan and I went to see the movie *Chocolat* six months or so ago. It's about the liberation of the people in a small French village, who've been oppressed by the Church – especially the Church's clergy – for generations. They've lost their joie de vivre. They've lost the freedom to be and to become. They've lost even the sense of the love and forgiveness of God. Having to be "good" has killed their spirits. But a chocolatier, a single woman, and her daughter blow into the village and open up a candy shop, right at the beginning of Lent. The mayor of the village, who's the enforcer of the doctrine and discipline of the parish church and the whole community, immediately concludes that this unbeliever – this witch! – is the enemy of his people. She will corrupt them with pleasure. So he wages a campaign to run her out of business and, if possible, out of the village. In the end, however, she prevails. She, free-spirited, spontaneous, non-judgmental, tolerant, affirming of everybody's humanity, fearless in the face of opposition, begins to set the people free, first one, then another, beginning with the most condemned and ostracized. Finally, ironically, she sets the young callow, timid parish priest free, too. On Easter Day, he climbs up into the pulpit that's so high all you can think of is the judgment seat of Almighty God; and he throws away the sermon the mayor has written for him and ad libs his own. This is what he says: "We can't go around measuring our goodness by what we don't do, by what we deny ourselves, by what we resist, by whom we exclude. We ought to measure our goodness by what we embrace, by what we create, by whom we include."

I was so thrilled by that sermon that Jan and I went straight from the theater to a bookstore, to buy a copy of *Chocolat*. We had no trouble finding a copy at Barnes & Noble. Standing there in the bookstore, hushed and hallowed as a library, I began reading the last chapter of the novel, hoping to find that sermon. (It's not there, by the way. It's only in the screenplay.) This little kid, maybe five or six years old, came running down the aisle, arms outstretched as if he were an airplane, making the sound of jet engines, "Rrrrrrr." When he got to where I was, he banked a little, to avoid a collision with me, then peeled off into non-fiction. I knew right away who it was. It was the ascending Christ, heaven-bound.

Final story.

Not many months ago, I went to the Eckstein Center – that's a hospice – to visit a parishioner who was dying. He was dying from a brain disease that the doctors at the Mayo Clinic Hospital never conclusively diagnosed. It was probably Bovine Spongiform Encephalopathy. It was awful, whatever it was. Though he was a retired colonel in the Air Force, he wasn't very old. He was a fighter pilot; and, when he was stationed in England, a squadron commander. He was happily married. He had a great job. Then, all of a sudden, this. I pushed open the door of his darkened room; and there he was, the man who, in only eight weeks, had been wasted by a virulent and merciless disease. He lay on his back, his arms hanging off the bed, his head to one side. Cruciform he was. And I suspect that, if he was thinking anything, he was thinking, "Eli, Eli, lama sabachthani… My God, my God, why hast thou forsaken me?" I felt as if I were standing, not just at the foot of this man's bed, but also at the foot of the cross of Christ.

I don't know what you're thinking about all of this – but I know what you could be thinking. You could be thinking, "This is the sappiest Christology I've ever heard. Bishop Thornton lives in a fantasy world. He doesn't have a clue about the transcendence of God." Well, let me tell you something. There are lots of things I don't have a clue about. But I'll tell you something else. If I didn't maintain this confusion about the people who come into my life, I'd just become more self-obsessed and more disinterested in and more unconcerned about and more unresponsive to other human beings than I already am. I'd become the worst of all things, hard-hearted; and I'd be utterly useless to God. So I have to work at it; and I can't tell you how many times I lapse and never recognize people's essential dignity, they who bear the image of God. But, when I'm not lapsing, this is what I do: face-to-face with another person, I say, as the medieval theologians and mystics said, "This is Thou, but

Thou art not this." Say it. "This is Thou, but Thou art not this." By maintaining this constant bafflement, that's how I find the Risen Christ on two feet in this world — and, I suspect, that's how the Risen Christ finds me, too.

The Rt. Rev. John S. Thornton
St. Mary's Episcopal Church
Eugene, Oregon
April 21, 2002

# "No" To The "Devil" Is "Yes" To God

"It is no longer I who live, but Christ
who lives in me."

So Paul wrote to the Christians in Galatia. Down the centuries, many Christians would agree with him. Many wouldn't. Lucky for Paul – and lucky for all of us – none of us is Paul's or anybody else's judge. One thing is indisputable, however: Paul set the right goal for every Christian. What we hope to say one day is that "it is no longer (we) who live, but Christ who lives in (us)."

Many of you seem old enough to remember that great western movie called *Pale Rider.* However, maybe many of you haven't seen it. Clint Eastwood is the "pale rider." Actually, he isn't at all pale; he's ruddy and weather-beaten. It's his horse who's pale as a ghost and very beautiful. The minute the horse and rider come on the scene, you know, you just know, that they're straight out of the Book of Revelation. "And there, as I looked, was another horse, sickly pale; and its rider's name was Death, and Hades came close behind." (Revelation 6:8.) (Isn't the Book of Revelation fun?) You also know that the rider, being Clint Eastwood, is a fearsome and notorious gunslinger, the kind you'd shoot only if he had his back turned to-ward you – and maybe not even then. But he doesn't have any guns!!! He isn't armed and he isn't, apparently, dangerous. Somewhere along the way, he has gotten religion – and, furthermore, he has gotten himself ordained. One night, at supper in a mining camp in Carbon Canyon, he turns up wearing an Anglican clerical collar. By God – I'm speaking theologically now – by God, he's an Episcopalian. (Oh, how I wish we had clergy like that, whose very presence would make people prefer the ways of righteousness and holiness.) Everybody calls him "Preacher," though he doesn't do any preaching and apart from a brief, very brief, grace at the table, very little praying. He's a man of few words, but every word he utters comes out of some deep place in his still troubled, still unresolved, still yet-to-be-fully-converted soul. At least, he's armed with a Bible, not with six-guns.

Here's the situation. The "bad guys" have exhausted the veins of gold and eroded the land by hydraulic mining in their claims. The only good place left to mine is in Carbon Canyon, where the "good guys" have set up a tent camp and are slowly and laboriously panning for gold, with limited success. So, to take control over the canyon, the bad guys have to drive the good guys out, by threatening them and by terrorizing them and, finally, by destroying their tent camp and shooting their Jersey milk cow and a teenage girl's beloved dog. It's Gold Country war. Obviously, Clint Eastwood is there to save the good guys. And the boss of the bad guys, Mr. Coy, is intuitive enough and Machiavellian enough and just plain mean enough to know that he has to find a way to "buy" that preacher. In town to get some supplies one day, Preacher is invited to Mr. Coy's office. Mr. Coy's son and his foreman and half a dozen of his goons are there, to protect the boss and to watch the preacher trade the lives of the miners for Mr. Coy's idea of a preacher's "success." (I have an eye for all tales about attempts to corrupt the clergy.) This is how the dialogue goes. I'll play both parts.

"Preacher, my name is Coy."

"I know."

(Mr. Coy gets a bottle of bourbon and two glasses.)

"Do you imbibe?"

"Only after nine in the morning."

"When I heard a parson was comin' to town, I had an image of a pale, scrawny, Bible-thumpin' easterner, with a linen handkerchief and bad lungs."

"That's me."

"Hardly."

(Mr. Coy gives Preacher a glass of bourbon, then raises his glass, to toast him.)

"Your health, sir. You know, it occurred to me that it must be difficult for a man of faith to carry the message on an empty stomach, so to speak. So I thought, 'Why not invite this devout and humble man to preach in town? Why not let the town be his parish? In fact, why not build him a brand new church?'"

"Well, I can see that a preacher would be mighty tempted by an offer like that."

"Oh, indeed."

"First thing you'd know he'd be thinkin' about getting himself a batch of new clothes."

"Why, we'd have 'em tailor-made."

"Then he'd start thinkin' about those Sunday collections."

"Hell, in a town as rich as this, that preacher, well, he'd be a wealthy man."

"That's why it wouldn't work. You can't serve God and Mammon."

Mr. Coy is stunned – and furious. Nobody doesn't go along with Mr. Coy. Nobody lectures Mr. Coy on religion. His religion is Mammon. His religion is brute force. His religion is total disregard for the lives of other human beings.

Isn't "Coy" the perfect name for the "Devil?" Whenever I use the word "Devil," I put it in quotes. It's a metaphor. It can be anyone who tempts us to betray our neighbors...or ourselves...or God. It could be we ourselves who tempt others to do just that. But Preacher is wise to Mr. Coy, to the tempter. Apparently, he is, as Paul said, "rooted and grounded" in the Gospel of Jesus Christ. "You can't serve God and Mammon." Good for that preacher with the Anglican clerical collar. He's dressed for virtue.

Every time we gather for Eucharist, we say the Confession. It's always time to be honest about ourselves. Jesus had to be, too. After his baptism, he went into the wilderness, to fast and to pray. He was there for a long time, forty days and forty nights, according to the text and to tradition. He had to find out if he had a will apart from and contrary to God's will. You know that best in moments of weakness, physical and emotional and spiritual and moral weakness, because that's when the "devil" comes to you, making suggestions that, in your weakness, don't seem particularly outrageous. C'mon, if you're the Son of God, turn these stones into bread. C'mon, if you're the Son of God, jump off the pinnacle of the Temple and float to the ground in the arms of angels. C'mon, if you're the Son of God, take over the world with your charisma; and when your charisma runs out, use power and force and violence. Don't accept the limitations of your humanity. Stuff like that can get into your head, unless, of course, only God is in your head, for which reason Jesus could say, "But it is written…"…"But it is written…"…"But it is written…." When you know the divine wisdom and the divine imperative, you also know the divine answer. The divine answer is "No…no, no, no."

According to "The Definition of the Divine and Human Natures in the Person of Christ," formulated by the Council of Chalcedon in 451 A.D., Jesus was "like us in all respects, apart from sin…." I subscribe to that – but, sometimes, I have my doubts. I don't doubt the "apart from sin" part; I doubt the "like us in all respects" part. I'm sure that, in many respects, he wasn't at all like me and I'm not at all like him. I'll give you an example. From the cross, instead of damning them all to hell, he forgave them all. Would I do that? Possibly, as Clint Eastwood does in *Pale Rider*, I'd go to the bank, get my six-guns out of a safe deposit box, drop my Anglican collar into it and go out and blow them all away. Well, I wouldn't do that, since I don't have any guns or a safe deposit box – or the desire or the will or anything that would motivate me to blow them all away, just as the pale rider does (and had to do, since it's a western). However, I would fantasize about it.

Preacher just couldn't stay in the Christ role; he had to resort to violence. Had to. He believed in what's called "redemptive violence," which is hardly more than the lust for revenge. In a world of violence, we're all tempted to get out of the Christ role. As for me, I'm trying to do a little better, be a little more like my Savior and Lord, who had what Archbishop William Temple called that "splendid incapacity for evil." That's because Jesus, in his freedom, chose not to have a will apart from God's will. I don't have that "splendid incapacity" yet. I'd like to have it. I'd like to think I'm striving for it. And maybe the best way to strive for it is not to strive for it at all, but simply to remember God at every moment and in every circumstance.

The Hasidim of Eastern Europe used to say that "sin" is simply "forgetting God." When we forget God, we're easy prey for the "Devil." I don't know how we can possibly cope with all the temptations that are laid before us every day, day after day after day, except by repeating, "God the Father above me, God the Son beside me, God the Holy Spirit in me" and staying close to the people who love God and who talk about their love for God and act as though their love for God is above all other loves. It's having our hearts constantly prepared to say "No" to the "Devil," which is always "Yes" to God.

I love that third stanza of "Ein Feste Burg" ("A Mighty Fortress is our God").

"And tho' this world, with devils filled,
Should threaten to undo us;
We will not fear, for God hath willed
His truth to triumph through us;
The Prince of Darkness grim,
We tremble not for him;
His rage we can endure,
For lo! His doom is sure,
One little word shall fell him."

"One little word shall fell him." You know what that one little word is? It's "No." N – o. No. That's all, but it's everything. That one little word can only come from vast hearts vastly prepared to say "Yes" to God, to "God the Father above (us), to God the Son beside (us), to God the Holy Spirit in (us)." It is in such moments that we realize that "it is no longer (we) who live, but Christ who lives in (us)."

The Rt. Rev. John S. Thornton
St. Michael's Cathedral
Boise, Idaho
June 16, 2013

# Nor The Hope Of The Poor Be Taken Away

V. Let not the needy, O Lord, be forgotten;

R. Nor the hope of the poor be taken away.

—⚉—

That's a Versicle and the Response from Suffrages A in Morning Prayer in *The Book of Common Prayer.* You're not going to leave this church before you've memorized the words of the response. I'll say, "Let not the needy, O Lord, be forgotten;" and you'll say, "Nor the hope of the poor be taken away." Let's do it. Let's do it again. One more time.

There are all kinds of ways to be poor. There are as many ways to be poor as there are people in the world. You can be poor in money, food, clothing, housing, as millions are. (However, I'm reminded of something Seneca, the Roman philosopher, said: "It is not the man who has too little, but the man who craves more who is poor.") You can be poor in education. You can be poor in opportunities. You can be poor in worthwhile, fulfilling employment. You can be poor in the welcome and acceptance and approval of the community, just because there's something different about you. You can be poor in an appropriate, moral, healthy self-love. You can be poor in the satisfaction of knowing that, at the end, you've done something good for humankind. (I noticed that Mikhail Kalashnikov, an Orthodox Christian, the inventor of the AK-47, the world's most popular firearm, a hundred million of them around to kill with, shortly before his death wrote, "The pain in my soul is unbearable.") You can be poor in physical or emotional or spiritual health. And you can be poor in life without a continual resurrecting, death-be-damned meaning.

One of the worst things we can do is to take away the hope of the poor.

A few weeks ago, Jan and I went to *Nebraska*. In fact, we went twice. I don't mean the state Nebraska; I mean the movie *Nebraska*. It's a parable about not taking away the hope of the poor. It's not a comedy, but parts of it are comical; it's not a tragedy, though pathos hangs over it, darkly, as at a time without the memory of fall or the surety of spring.

Woodrow ("Woody") Grant is a "cranky ol' coot." Eighty years old. Korean War vet. Retired as a partner in a garage and gas station in Hawthorne, Nebraska. Married (to Kate) necessarily, habitually, robotically. Uncommunicative, doesn't speak in paragraphs, even sentences, just growls a word or two. Drinks too much; okay, a drunk. (He justifies himself by saying to his son David, "If you were married to your mother, you'd drink, too.") In spite of anything that might be said about Woody Grant, little of it, maybe none of it flattering, he's a person, God's person, God's begotten son somehow. Somehow. For those who are perfect, it must be a low-class, shameless God.

However, suddenly, Woody is a man with some hope for the future. He has just gotten a mailing proclaiming him the winner of the million dollar sweepstakes prize. "Pay to the order of Woodrow

Grant $1,000,000.00." Nothing will stop him from going from his home in Billings, Montana to Lincoln, Nebraska, to collect the money. He'll walk if he has to. He'll walk 900 miles if he has to. And he has to. Nobody's going to take him there. Everybody else knows it's a hoax. You have to buy magazines to be eligible for the prize. He hasn't bought any magazines. He hasn't read the fine print. But it says he's the winner; so he's going to Lincoln if it's the last thing he does on this earth. He doesn't want to be rich, invest in stocks and bonds and real estate and travel. He just wants a new pickup truck and a new air compressor. That's all. His life would be complete.

In one scene, his wife, Kate, is overheard telling their older son, Ross, "If I had a million dollars, I'd put him in a home." That's exactly what Ross would do, too. A few minutes later, Ross, who believes that his dad is addled and sodden beyond redemption and in need of being warehoused, speaks uncompromisingly to his younger brother, David. David listens, until his brother's unlove compels his advocacy for their father. "He has to have something to give his life meaning!" Now that's the voice of God and of God's Christ. "I have come that you may have life and have it abundantly." How can we live without the conviction that there's Someone out there who insists upon the best that's in us, Someone whose insistence keeps us wide-eyed and breathless?

In the Twentieth Century, the most popular book checked out of the New York Public Library was Viktor Frankl's *Man's Search for Meaning.* Evidently, millions of Americans needed to learn or to be reminded that, without some surpassing meaning, our lives can run down to little more than hanging on for dear life – and, sometimes, thinking that life's not all that dear and, maybe, wishing it was over.

Frankl spoke from experience. The original title of the book was *From Death Camp to Existentialism*. He was in a death camp, one affiliated with Dachau. He observed that some people just died, of no apparent cause, essentially of hopelessness. But the Nazis couldn't starve the meaning of life out of others, couldn't work the meaning of life out of others, couldn't beat the meaning of life out of others. Sustained by Judaism, they knew that no person, no party, no nation could ever evade the judgment of God and that there would be a future and salvation.

For Woody Grant, the hope of getting a new pickup truck and a new air compressor with his winnings was the future and was, in a funny way, salvation.

During the stopover in Hawthorne, Woody and Kate and their two sons visit the farm where Woody grew up. The place is as gray as the gray winter sky, as grave as the dead grass around it. The farmhouse is abandoned now. Doors are off their hinges, windows are broken, probably smashed for the fun of it by kids in the evening. Pieces of furniture, like the bones of a dead household, lie scattered around. The four of them walk from room to room, but they're as silent as the wheat stubble in the neighbor's distant fields. Once upstairs, in what was his parent's bedroom, Woody speaks for the first time. "Whenever I came into this room," he says, "I was whipped." That explains it, the joylessness, the resentment as hard as the frozen ground, the cold fear of those who only demand and command, only criticize and censure, only humiliate and shame, only punish, having the power of the hand or the paddle or the switch. How can you grow up without play, without tenderness, without praise, without big bear hugs and wet smacks and I-love-you's? You can't. You grow down into a tenth of what, with affirmation, you might have become.

Like Woody, you can shuffle through life, but you can't dance. We've been ordained to dance. And according to ancient wisdom, the truth is in the dance, in the graceful movement among others who cherish the collaborative footwork of freedom.

Ross, the older son, a local TV news anchor, has little empathy for his dad. David, a struggling electronics salesman, has a better understanding of the struggle for a life with meaning. He decides to take some days off and drive his dad to Lincoln, knowing that the rainbow's end wouldn't be at the Cornhusker Promotions office. Kate persuades them to go as far as Hawthorne on the first day and stay with relatives. They agree, though they dread it, like dreading going to a graveyard at night. Still, it would save money.

The attitudes and ideas and feelings of the relatives are as unmoved and fixated as the furniture in the front room of Woody's sister's house. Like that furniture, the furnishings of their inner lives are frayed and soiled, worn into a comfortable drabness. And why not? The whole town is depressed and futureless. There's an emptiness there, but the emptiness is filled with sorrows. But when the relatives and, soon, all the townspeople learn that Woody, good ol' Woody, has won a million dollars, they perk up. They want to believe it. They need to believe it. It could be life for them too. And they come up with reasons why Woody owes them something. (Pray that you'll never win the lottery. It's like being attacked by a swarm of killer bees.) Greed becomes absolutely corpuscular, making them tingle with anticipation of some kind of payback.

That's especially true with Ed, Woody's former partner in the garage and gas station. Ed's a bully. If there's a "satanic" person in town, it's Ed. By his reckoning, Woody owes him money. Ten thousand dollars. In one scene, he bellies David up against the sink in the men's room in the restaurant and explains, menacingly, that, if Woody doesn't come up with the money, there could be legal action. (Lawyers must hate being used as the agents of vengeance.) In another scene, in the same restaurant, with Woody himself present, Ed tells David about Woody's affair with an Indian woman from a nearby reservation before David was born. That's how you do it, satanically. To get an advantage over another person, you find ways to take his dignity away, so that you look good and he looks evil. After all, ten thousand dollars is infinitely more valuable than another man's dignity, isn't it?

It's the habit of humans – and God isn't in that humanity – to collect information about each other...and keep it to themselves...until it's to their advantage to use it. It doesn't have to be an open accusation when an insinuation will do. What we can and sometimes do, on a much smaller scale, though no less satanic, is like the blood sport of American politics. We have to be vigilant about our own behavior.

David and Woody do, finally, get to Lincoln, to the Cornhusker Promotions office. A young woman, with a kind of precocious understanding of the befuddlements of the naïve, explains that Woody's number isn't the winning number. However, would he like a hat that says "Winner" on it? He would. In a sense, he has won. He has won the truth about the world. With a kind of sadness, the young woman says to David, "Some people believe everything they read." But, above all, Woody has won the love of his son David.

The movie does have a sweet ending. On the way back to Billings, David trades his Subaru Outback for a Ford Explorer pickup and buys a Craftsman air compressor. When they get to Hawthorne, David lets his dad drive down the main street, "Winner" hat on his head. The people on the street gawk and wave and, all except Ed, quietly celebrate Woody's victory.

It's true love that makes such things happen. In *Nebraska*, it's David's true love for his father, not a love he always felt, but a love he grew into. It's love full of the knowledge that everybody's imperfect, say "sinful" if you want to or must…full of the patience that will suffer exasperation and costs something…full of the understanding of what it might be like to be the other person…full of the forgiveness based, largely, on the realization of your own underserved forgiveness, in spite of all the things you wish not to remember…full of the hope of everybody's resurrection in this life in this world, right up to the last breath, then for eternity.

We are the people who, having been given the hope of the resurrection, give hope to those who, in whatever ways they're poor, have no hope. We do for them what Christ has done for us. As Christ gave his life for the life of the world, so we do the same.

"Let not the needy, O Lord, be forgotten."
"Nor the hope of the poor be taken away."

The Rt. Rev. John S. Thornton
St. Michael's Cathedral
Boise, Idaho
January 26, 2014

# The Christ Child And The Farm Set

This is a reminiscence from childhood. Though it's in three parts, it's a continuous reflection on that story.

## Part I

A week or ten days before Christmas 1937 – though it might have been 1936 – our parents took us to a department store in Richmond, Indiana "to look at the decorations." We were living in Cambridge City, a small town about thirty-five miles west on Highway 40. It was an all-day expedition. Our mother made sandwiches, peanut butter and jelly, Velveeta cheese, which we ate in the car along the way. Because Christmas was only days away, we children, three of us, two boys, one girl, were unusually well-behaved. No pinching, no poking, no provoking our parents' censure or, as it always turned out, no idle threat to put us out of the car and make us walk home. This time, they might even have been proud.

"Looking at the decorations" meant that my brother and sister and I would, first, look at the decorations, with a degree of bedazzlement, then, of course, look for the toys. It was the biggest department store we had ever seen, vastly bigger than the general store diagonally across the street from the Methodist church on the main street in Cambridge City. It was so big that it had an escalator from the first to the second floor. One would be whisked up, one would float down. Up and down we went. Up and Down. Up and Down. We were whisked up to the second heaven of home furnishings and appliances and linens — and toys! — and floated down again to the first heaven of cosmetics and jewelry and women's and girls' clothing and men's and boys' clothing. Once our eyes had adjusted to the gloss and glitter and glare of that heavenly emporium, we began chasing each other up the "DOWN" escalator, then down the "UP" escalator. A floorwalker, just as obvious as a cop on a beat, watched us for a while, then gave us that "look." Since we were schoolchildren, we knew the meaning of that "look" and quickly transformed ourselves into angels. To evade the wrath of the floorwalker *and* the wrath of God — after all, we were Calvinists — *and*, of course, the displeasure of Santa Claus, we rode the escalator up to the second floor and vanished into "TOYS." It was there that I saw it. I was transfixed by it. I was entranced by it. I felt a tremor of excitement such as I had never felt before. It was the one thing I wanted. Nothing else attracted me or diverted my attention or made me think twice about my heart's desire. I didn't want an electric train. I didn't want roller skates. I didn't want a bicycle. I didn't want Lincoln Logs. I just wanted that. I wanted that farm set. It had two brown rubber Percheron draft horses, two black and white rubber Holstein milk cows, two black and white rubber Hampshire pigs, two white rubber Merino sheep, six red rubber Rhode Island Red chickens, a red metal Farmall "H" tractor, a red metal hay wagon and a red wooden barn with a hip roof and sliding doors. You could take the roof off the barn and look down into the hayloft and the horse stalls and the milking parlor. I was stupefied by wonder — by a blatant and irrepressible desire to have that farm set. I was hardly aware that my parents had come up behind me.

Our parents told us children to meet them downstairs, by the front door, in ten minutes. One after the other, we floated down the escalator, I backwards, hoping. And though our parents left the store with armloads of bags and boxes, so far as I knew, they left without the farm set.

## Part II

A few days before Christmas, I went out to the garage to build a birdhouse out of scrap lumber. I thought our mother would like a birdhouse for Christmas. If not, some mother bird probably would. Our father had a workbench and a tool chest in the garage, and there was a box full of scraps nearby. I'd never built a birdhouse before. Never built anything before. Didn't have a plan. Of course, to keep it all a secret, I couldn't ask for any guidance. The vice worked okay, but sawing…and sawing…and sawing just got to be too much. I gave up. And where were the nails? I'd have to make something out of construction paper instead. We'd done that in school. It could be a stable maybe, with a manger made from ice cream bar sticks or tongue depressors.

The car was in the garage, a Dodge from the late 20s. The Christmas presents were brought home in that car. I saw my parents put everything in the trunk. Maybe they were still there. The trunk wasn't locked. I turned the handle and opened it. There, in the semi-darkness of the rear of the trunk it was, the farm set. I slammed that trunk shut and went jubilantly, though guiltily, into the house, trying to look innocent of my discovery, with no way to thank my parents until Christmas Day.

From the moment I slammed that trunk shut against my sight, I've known exactly who attended the birth of our Lord: two brown Percheron draft horses, two black and white rubber Holstein milk cows, two black and white Hampshire pigs, two white Merino sheep, six red Rhode Island Red chickens and my parents, who, a high school agriculture teacher and basketball coach and his wife, in the midst of America's Great Depression, felt the desire of my heart and spent more than they should have, spent themselves really, to fulfill it.

So that is how desire works. You desire a thing with all your heart, until your heart aches; then someone who loves you feels that desire and desires it with you and for you, until his or her heart aches too. Then, for the satisfaction of it, for pure delight, for everlasting joy, he or she gives it.

## Part III

So that is how desire works.

If I should desire the things of Christ for myself until my heart aches, would the God of Love give them to me?

"How silently, how silently,
the wondrous gift is given!
So God imparts to human hearts
the blessings of His heaven..."

How silently they will be given to me – and you – those wondrous gifts, if you and I desire them.

Desire the gift of always having only one motive, to love, to love those who are easy to love, to love those who, for you, are hard to love.

Desire the gift of thankfulness in any and every circumstance, even when you can't think of a good reason for doing so.

Desire the gift of humility before the majesty of the mountains and the majesty hidden in the hearts of ordinary people.

Desire the gift of trust in the mysterious purpose and power of God in the events of the passing days.

Desire the gift of gentleness in every glance and in every word and with every touch of the hand.

Desire the gift of joy in simply being alive and joy in being alive in Christ and joy in knowing that death will not be the victor.

Desire the gift of forgiveness as it makes all things new for those growing old in guilt or shame or fear.

Desire the gift of peace in heart and home and homeland and the whole inhabited world.

Desire them all and many more until your heart aches, so that you may become the flesh of God's desire for a new humanity in the likeness of Christ.

The Rt. Rev. John S. Thornton
St. Michael's Cathedral
Boise, Idaho
December 22, 2013

# Virgin Birth: Or The Fathering Of God

This isn't a sermon; it's a story – about half of the original – that I wrote at Christmas in 1984. It's titled *Virgin Birth: Or the Fathering of God*. This story isn't historical...isn't biblical...isn't traditional... isn't meant to question or doubt the Nativity stories in Matthew and Luke. It's entirely novelistic. However, it's also entirely logical. My dogmatic belief is that Joseph had to have had a lot to do with the formation of the personality and character and values *and* nerve of Jesus. This story is meant to acknowledge and honor that certainty. We're all formed in relationships...and reformed in relationships... and transformed in our relationship to Jesus Christ.

But, first, you need to know something about this story. In it, Joseph is a dreamer. In many of his dreams, not out of nowhere, but from somewhere deep within himself, comes a luminous figure, vivid, almost tangible, who, with congenial command, encourages him never to be afraid to be like the Father, like "Abba," the Father. Joseph calls him his "archangel."

I begin with the first sentence of the story, which is repeated at the end, then skip three and a half pages.

It didn't happen at night at all. It happened shortly before noon, on a Wednesday...

The days went by.

About ten days before they had to leave for Bethlehem, between three and four in the morning, Joseph sat straight up in bed, right out of a sound sleep. He stretched his arms. He rubbed his eyes. He sighed long and deep, until he was breathless and tingling. He flopped down again, bouncing Mary to wakefulness. With fat fingers, he combed her soft hair and, then, laid his huge hand lightly on her bulging belly. "Mary," he whispered, "it isn't a girl."

"Huh?"

"I said it isn't a girl. It's a boy. A boy!" he shouted, forgetting how much he had wanted a girl.

"How can you possibly know a thing like that?" she asked, now wide-awake.

"The archangel told me so. He was here, just a few minutes ago, and he said, 'Joseph, you're going to have a son.' And do you know what else he said?"

"I can't imagine."

He said, "You have to name him Joshua. Don't name him anything else."

"Joshua! Joseph, we could name him after you. What's wrong with your name? Or John, after my dad? Or…"

"Mary, we don't have a choice. The archangel meant what he said. I could tell."

"Okay, okay. Go back to sleep. We'll talk about it in the morning. I love you."

"His name's going to be Joshua," Joseph decreed, pulling Mary close to his burly body, gently.

Three weeks later, in Bethlehem, Mary gave birth to her baby, a boy. Seven pounds, four ounces. Twenty-one inches long. They named him "Joshua." But they called him "Josh."

And the weeks went by.

They were still at the inn, renting by the week. It really was a nice place, and the price was right. And, besides, the inn-keeper's wife, having had seven babies of her own, showed Mary all about taking care of little Josh, breast-feeding and burping and bathing and all that. She was a godsend. She even arranged for the local rabbi to do the circumcision. But this tiny paradise was blown to pieces one night, like a meteor hitting the earth. No sooner had they kissed goodnight than Joseph fell asleep, exhausted by a burden of vaguest anticipations. Mary lay awake, thinking it was about time they made plans to go back to Nazareth. It was she who felt the initial thud and the subsequent shock waves, as if the epicenter of some terrible happening were right there under the inn. Under the bed! Under the covers! The epicenter was Joseph, dreaming. He shook all over. "Joseph, Joseph," Mary said, patting him on the head, "Wake up." He felt that he had just been crushed by some heavy object that came plummeting out of the heavens.

"Mary, we have to get out of here."

"I've been thinking the same thing. The baby's old enough to travel now and..."

"Let's get packed, Mary. We're leaving right now. We're going to Egypt."

"Egypt?" she screamed, then covered her mouth. "Have you gone bonkers? There's nobody in Egypt but Egyptians. We're staying right here."

"Mary, listen to me. Please. The archangel was just here. He told me that Herod really has cracked up this time and that he's already sending his troops out to kill little boys. His horoscope said that a new king had been born right under his nose. So, we're checking out, Sweetie. Tonight!"

"I guess I have no choice," she sighed.

The innkeeper, though dazed, tried to be understanding about the abrupt departure. He always got up at two in the morning he said. Joseph paid him twice what was due, and he even left a little money for each of his seven kids. He thanked him profusely for everything he and his wife had done; and the innkeeper thanked him back, sincerely. Then the three of them, Joseph, Mary and Josh, just a bundle with a face, vanished into the darkness, heading south- southwest.

And the months went by.

Mary was wrong about Egypt. There weren't just Egyptians there. There were Jews, lots of Jews, from Palestine and everywhere. Joseph and Mary and Josh had landed right in the middle of a community of Jewish survivors. They had learned to get along quite nicely in a foreign country. They helped each other find work...and organized co-ops and day-care centers...and floated loans...and swapped recipes...and had street dances...and took chicken soup to sick folks... and hired their own rabbi, so they'd never forget Jerusalem. It wasn't a bad life for any of them. Joseph and Mary and Josh were happy there, and they almost lost their hankering for their homeland after a while. It wasn't surprising. Joseph became a huge success. He started out doing odd jobs for rich Egyptians. Then he was hired as a carpenter, fulltime. Then he set up his own construction business. And did he make money. With his personality and skills, it was bound to happen. And the three of them might have spent the rest of their lives there had it not been for another nighttime visitation. The archangel appeared and simply told Joseph to head for home. Herod, the old buzzard, was dead.

"Mary," he said, lying in bed with his hands under his head, "guess what?"

"The archangel came to you in the night?"

"How'd you guess? So if you are so smart, tell me what he said."

"He said, 'Joseph, head for home. Herod, the old buzzard, is dead.'"

"You're incredible," Joseph said, believing it with all his heart.

She was incredible. She didn't complain or even ask any questions. She trusted him and his archangel. But it was hard for her to leave her friends. And it took a while for him to close up the business.

The years went by.

Jimmy was born. And Zach. And Sam. Then a whole string of girls, beginning with Mildred and ending with Frieda, the last of twelve children. Joseph would have died for them, he loved them so much.

Joseph lived his whole life that way, waiting for his archangel to tell him what to say or do next, and then saying or doing it immediately, without a second thought, apparently oblivious to consequences. He seemed awfully impulsive. Not erratic. Or unpredictable and wild and scary. Not crazy. Just awfully impulsive. But Mary and the kids trusted him and those impulses, like they trusted the coming of the next day's dawn.

Joseph was, probably, the sweetest man in Nazareth. Probably in Galilee. Probably in Palestine. Possibly in the whole world. Everybody thought so. There wasn't anything he wouldn't do for people, friends or strangers. And he'd get the family and all the relatives and as many neighbors as he could to do things they never dreamed of. They'd feel so darned good afterward they'd think it was their own idea. He'd make them believe it was. But, if Joseph's sense of fairness or justice was ever violated, he could come on like Almighty God. He caught a couple of money changers trying to swindle this daffy old woman once. Do you know what he did? He picked up their table and threw the thing, probably, twenty-five or thirty feet. The whole town heard about it. And nobody ever forgot. He would have been loved for that alone.

And on and on.

Joseph became what not every man becomes: a hero to his wife and children...and relatives...and friends...and practically everybody who ever met him. He would have died for them, he loved them so much.

Finally, he did. He died. Joseph died. It was shortly before noon, on a Wednesday.

Mary wept and wept and wept. It was as if the Sun, Moon and stars had fallen out of the sky. It was the darkest day of her life and nobody could give her light.

The kids tried to be brave. But how can you be brave when bravery dies?

It was Mary's oldest child, her son Josh, who finally stopped the flood of tears. "You know, Mom," he said, "Dad always made me want to be like God."

The words came through the pain like a baby at birth.

The Rt. Rev. John S. Thornton
St. Michael's Cathedral
Boise, Idaho
January 5, 2014

# Namaan

I love this story about Namaan the Aramaean in 2 Kings 5. Now Namaan wasn't your average Aramaean. He was the commander of the king of Aram's army. He had come through the ranks, all the way from lugging spears for the real warriors to becoming the most powerful – and famous – military man, not only in Aram, but also in all the kingdoms in that part of the world. (I'm making much of this up. It doesn't say any of that in the Bible. However, it's logical.) Namaan was fearless. With his bare hands or rocks or clubs or swords or spears, he was indomitable. And he didn't just order his men into battle; he led his men into battle and stayed with them until the battle was over – and won. They never lost. So the word went out: Don't mess with Aram. The Aramaeans lived with a sense of security, mostly because of Namaan and his army. Whenever the general drove his chariot through the city, crowds would gather and shout, "Namaan! Namaan! Namaan!" (Note: Here the congregation, on cue, shouts, "Namaan! Namaan! Namaan!" to get viscerally involved in the sermon.) As for the king, he was terribly grateful to the general and rewarded him in every way he could. There wasn't anything the general and Mrs. Namaan needed. They had chefs and housekeepers and gardeners and horse trainers and groomers and slaves to clean out the stables and everything. The general and his wife didn't have to lift a finger. (You won't find any of this in an English Bible. You have to read the Hebrew text, which usually says pretty much what I want it to say.) There was only one thing that kept Namaan from luxuriating in it all and from utter contentment. He was a leper. The commander of the king of Aram's army was a leper! There were ugly, oozing, bloody sores all over his extremities, his arms, his legs, his feet. Ugh!!!

Israel was just across the border from Aram. The Aramaeans had things that the Israelites wanted and needed, badly. It wasn't all "milk and honey" over there. So every once in a while, the Israelite army would march across the border; and, each time, they'd be driven back. The Aramaeans were fed up with it. The king was too. So was Namaan. When the Israelites crossed the border just one time too many, Namaan and his army went after them, all the way into their territory, all the way to Jerusalem; and, well, the only word that describes what the Aramaeans did to the Israelites is "slaughter." Then they plundered the place. And they took a whole slave-labor force back home with them. One of the slaves was a girl who was put to work in the general's household. She got lucky. So did Mrs. Namaan. The general, too. That girl had some very, very important information to share with them.

Once the girl found out that the general was a leper, she told Mrs. Namaan about the prophet in Samaria who could cure all kinds of diseases. There was no doubt in her mind that he could cure the general's leprosy. Mrs. Namaan told the general; and the general told the king, who said, "Get going! I'll write a letter to the king of Israel for you." So Namaan and his charioteers and servants took off for Jerusalem, with buckets of money ("ten talents of silver" and "six thousand shekels of gold") and a huge wardrobe ("ten sets of garments") to pay for the cure. In a rumble of chariot wheels and a clamor of snorts and whinnies, they rolled up to the king of Israel's palace. After that last slaughter, the Israelites weren't about to object to the presence of their enemy. Namaan's chief of staff leapt out of his chariot and hustled into the king's chamber with the letter from the king of Aram. It read: "When this letter reaches you, know that

I have sent to you my servant Namaan, that you may cure him of his leprosy." What a nice letter. You'd think that the king of Israel would have been relieved that that's all it was about. Instead, he went into a tizzy. Cure the commander of Aram's army of leprosy?! Who does he think I am? God? Then he really flipped out. He's trying to set me up for failure so he can kill me!!! He paced up and down and whined and wept over his fate and ripped his clothes, until he too was in need of a cure. And, by golly, he got one. The prophet in Samaria, Elisha, who got wind of all this, sent a runner to the king with this message: "Cool it!" (That's a loose translation of the Hebrew word, but that's pretty much what it means.) "I can cure him. By God, he'll learn that there's a prophet in Israel!" Off Namaan and his entourage went, to consult with this Elisha in Samaria, to the great relief of the king of Israel.

Not that everything up to this point hasn't been dramatic, but what comes next is high drama. General Namaan and his entourage pull up to Elisha's house. The dialogue between Namaan's chief of staff and Elisha might have gone something like this:

**Chief of staff**: "Hello. Hello? Hello!!"

**Elisha**: "Oh, hello out there."

**Chief of staff**: "General Namaan is out here. He's come all the way from Aram to see you. All the way."

**Elisha**: "Welcome. The king told me that he'd be coming. Understand that he's got a bad skin disease. Most likely leprosy, huh?"

**Chief of staff**: "That's right. And he sure needs your help."

**Elisha**: "That's what I'm here for."

**Chief of staff**: "And the general is ready to pay you for your services, in silver and gold – and an awful lot of it. Some dandy clothes too."

**Elisha**: "He can keep all that. I don't charge anything. Does he think I'm corrupt? I do everything only for the glory of the God of Israel."

**Chief of staff**: "Really? You'd do this for nothing?"

**Elisha**: "No, not for nothing. For the glory of the God of Israel."

**Chief of staff**: "Can you come out and take a good look at the general?"

**Elisha**: "Don't need to. I know all about him. Just tell him to go down to the Jordan and dip himself in it seven times. Not six, mind you. Or eight. Seven times, and he'll be cured."

**Chief of staff**: "How about coming out and saying some prayers for him?"

**Elisha**: "That's all I've been doing since I learned about his condition."

**Chief of staff**: "At least, you could come out and wave your hands over him, couldn't you?"

**Elisha**: "That's not necessary. Just tell him to go down to the Jordan and dip himself in it seven times."

**Chief of staff**: "Do you realize that we have rivers in Aram? Isn't one river as good as another?"

**Elisha**: "No, all rivers aren't the same. The Jordan is special. That's my prescription. Take it or leave it."

**Chief of staff**: "You must understand that the general isn't accustomed to taking orders. He gives them."

**Elisha**: "I do understand, but he'd be smart to take orders this time."

**Chief of staff**: "And you're aware that the general is the most feared military man in all this part of the world, aren't you?"

**Elisha**: "Don't try to bully me. Just tell him to do what he's told. For the last time, tell him to go down to the Jordan and dip himself in it seven times. GOODBYE."

Namaan, having overheard all this, is furious. No respect. No deference. No groveling before the mighty man of Aram. He started kicking the chariot wheels and flinging dust at the horses and cursing to high heaven, but his chief of staff intervened in the tantrum. "Please. Please. If the prophet had asked you to do something really difficult, you would have done it. As it turns out, he's just asking you to go down to the Jordan and dip yourself in it seven times. C'mon, it's worth a try." "Oh, okay." So Namaan swallows his pride and climbs into his chariot, and he and his men head south, toward the Jordan. A couple of days later, when they get there, Namaan strips – it's not a pretty sight – and wades into the Jordan and dips his sorry self in it, right up to his eyeballs, once…twice…three times…four times…five times…

six times…then seven times…and Holy!!! "His flesh was restored like flesh of a young boy." It worked, just like Elisha said it would.

This, obviously, is mythologized history, which doesn't mean it's untrue. With the characters involved, you can believe that something remarkable, astonishing, and miraculous occurred. We'll just have to leave it there. However, one of the truths that the story conveys is that when you meet a person who has the authority of divine love you'd be smart – saved, really – to do what he or she says.

In the 8ᵗʰ chapter of Matthew's Gospel, a centurion stationed in Capernaum begs Jesus to heal his sick servant. "He's in desperate shape," he says. "I have no right to ask you to do this, but, please, come with me." So he does. Jesus goes with the man who has absolute authority over a hundred Roman soldiers and his household slaves. Nobody says "No" to him – or "I'll think about it." – or "When I get around to it." – or anything but "Yes, sir!" For the sake of his sick servant, the centurion makes himself no better than a slave. Jesus, it says in the text, is "amazed" that the man who is like a king in Capernaum would freely give up his authority so that the man with the authority of divine love could freely act.

Each one of us is the authority in his or her own life. Autonomy, at least to me, is really, really important. I don't give up mine easily. Ask anybody. However, when I do act on my own authority, every once in a while I make a mess of things. I can make Hell for myself – and other people too. That may be true of you as well, though I have no doubt that you're more saintly than I. No doubt. But we all say that Jesus is the Christ…is the Messiah…is the Savior of the world…is the Redeemer of humankind…is the Word made flesh…is the incarnation of the love of God…is the Third Person of the eternal Trinity…and a lot of other terms to describe the man who has the authority of divine love. So why don't we just do what he commands? When Jesus commands us to bless those who curse us, why don't we do that? When Jesus commands us to do good to those who hate us, why don't we do that? When Jesus commands us to pray for those who abuse us, why don't we do that? When Jesus commands us to love our enemies, why don't we do that? When Jesus commands us to forgive, as the condition of our own forgiveness, why don't we do that? When Jesus commands us not to judge one another and not to condemn one another, why don't we do that?

We Christians have been saying the Nicene Creed since the Fourth Century. We don't have to look at the Prayer Book anymore. We can say it backwards. We can say it in our sleep. It's part of us. There's no doubt that we're Nicene Christians. BUT – this is, I suspect, a minority opinion – there's entirely too much emphasis on right thinking and not nearly enough emphasis on right acting. Every time we recite the Nicene Creed we ought to recite the Beatitudes, the action that should characterize the Christian followers of the Jewish Jesus. "Blessed" are they. Or "blest" are they. Or "happy" are they. All three words are perfectly good translations of the Greek word *makarioi*. The Jesus Seminar scholars argue, strongly that *makarioi* should be translated "congratulations." "Congratulations to the gentle! They will inherit the earth," for instance. And "Congratulations to those who work for peace! They will be known as the children of God." And on and on. I like that. However, I still prefer the old J.B. Phillips translation of the Beatitudes, which, now, we're going to recite. Look on the front of the bulletin. Slowly and quietly, let's say them together.

"HOW HAPPY ARE THE HUMBLE-MINDED, FOR THE KINGDOM OF HEAVEN IS THEIRS!"

"HOW HAPPY ARE THOSE WHO KNOW WHAT SORROW MEANS, FOR THEY WILL BE GIVEN COURAGE AND COMFORT!"

"HOW HAPPY ARE THOSE WHO CLAIM NOTHING, FOR THE WHOLE EARTH WILL BELONG TO THEM!"

"HOW HAPPY ARE THOSE WHO ARE HUNGRY AND THIRSTY FOR GOODNESS, FOR THEY WILL BE FULLY SATISFIED!"

"HOW HAPPY ARE THE MERCIFUL, FOR THEY WILL HAVE MERCY SHOWN TO THEM!"

"HOW HAPPY ARE THE UTTERLY SINCERE, FOR THEY WILL SEE GOD!"

"HOW HAPPY ARE THOSE WHO MAKE PEACE, FOR THEY WILL BE KNOWN AS SONS (AND DAUGHTERS) OF GOD!"

My loves, that's the new way of living in an old world. So…let's dip ourselves in it seven times a day, seven days a week, until we are a new flesh with a new spirit.

The Rt. Rev. John S. Thornton
St. Michael's Cathedral
Boise, Idaho
February 12, 2012

# The Fourth of July

The Old Testament lesson for the Seventh Sunday after Pentecost is the story of Naaman, the commander of the Aramean army. Nobody told him what to do. He told everybody what to do. Nobody was going to tell him what to do about...about his leprosy. Not even Elijah, who knew the cure. One man with an authority problem (Naaman) meets another without an authority problem (Elijah). Take it or leave it, General. Finally, after a tantrum, Naaman takes it. And Naaman is cured. It's a great story. It will have to wait.

But this is the Third of July. Tomorrow is the Fourth. It's time for speeches and parades and fireworks and John Phillip Souza marches and "The 1812 Overture" and, here we go, "America the Beautiful." Let's sing it.

> "O beautiful for spacious skies,
> For amber waves of grain,
> For purple mountain majesties
> Above the fruited plain!
> America! America!
> God shed his grace on thee,
> And crown thy good with brotherhood
> From sea to shining sea."

Now that's a dickens of a good hymn...and a dickens of a good creed...and a dickens of a good ecology.

I'm going to begin with a quiz: What happened on the Fourth of July 1776? Don't be too quick to answer it. I'll answer it for you. The Second Continental Congress, meeting in Philadelphia, only *adopted* – didn't sign – The Declaration of Independence. Here's the chronology:

On July 1ˢᵗ, the Second Continental Congress met.

On July 2ⁿᵈ, twelve of the thirteen colonies voted in favor of a motion for independence.

On July 2ⁿᵈ and 3ʳᵈ, the delegates debated and revised the language of the statement drafted by Thomas Jefferson.

On July 4ᵗʰ, they *adopted* it.

So how come all thirteen colonies didn't vote in favor? Answer: The New York delegates hadn't been authorized to vote in favor, though they did, on July 9ᵗʰ.

So when was The Declaration of Independence signed? Answer: Not until August 2ⁿᵈ. It took a couple of weeks just to get the document "engrossed" (i.e., written on parchment).

How many men – sorry, no women in that Congress – signed it? Answer: Fifty-six, most of them native born, though eight were born in England, Scotland, Wales and Ireland. I'll give you some of the more prominent names: John Hancock, Thomas Jefferson, Benjamin Harrison, Benjamin Rush, Benjamin Franklin, Samuel Adams and, don't forget, Matthew Thornton.

My favorite, of course, is Matthew Thornton, a physician, from New Hampshire, born in Ireland. You'll see his signature in the lower right-hand corner of the document. There wasn't enough room under the New Hampshire place.

This is what those men had the nerve to say:

"We hold these truths to be self-evident, that all men are created equal, that they are endowed, by their Creator, with certain unalienable Rights, that among these are Life, Liberty, and the pursuit of Happiness. That to secure these rights, Governments are instituted among Men, deriving their just powers from the consent of the governed...."

Now that is the critical issue in America, election cycle after election cycle. We will not revert to a king or a lifetime president (Alexander Hamilton's idea) over us. We will, messy as it is, govern ourselves through our representatives.

That brings me to George Mason, the principal author of "The Declaration of Rights," which was adopted, unanimously, by the Fifth Virginia Convention on June 12th, 1776.

(George Mason was an Episcopalian. He and George Washington and George William Fairfax were all vestrymen of Truro Parish – at the same time! Can you imagine it? Though George Washington was on the building committee, his greater interest was in building a new nation.)

The Virginia "Declaration of Rights" was, in many ways, the basis for "The Declaration of Independence," adopted twenty-two days later. Thomas Jefferson leaned on it while drafting "The Declaration of Independence." And James Madison did as well, while drafting "The Bill of Rights" (introduced in 1789 and ratified in 1791).

There are sixteen articles in "The Declaration of Rights." (It should have said, "of individual citizens," though there were no rights whatsoever for slaves, whom many of those founders owned, in the tens and hundreds.)

I refer you, especially, to Article 16, the last of them: "That religion, or the duty which we owe to our Creator, and the manner of discharging it, can be directed only by reason and conviction, not by force or violence; and therefore all men are equally entitled to the free exercise of religion...." That means, equally, Episcopalians, Presbyterians, Methodists, Quakers, Mennonites, Catholics, Jews, Muslims (slaves, most of them) and on and on.

In the fall of 1784, Virginia's General Assembly debated whether or not to establish a religion. The presenting issue was a bill that would levy a general assessment for the support of the "Teachers of Religion." The Presbyterian clergy loved the idea. The Presbyterian laity hated it. They'd lose power over the clergy. Better to keep them on their payroll – and remove them as needed. The Methodists were split, for the same reasons the Presbyterians were. Of course, the Episcopalians were too. The clergy thought it was a good idea, getting everybody in Virginia to pick up their bills, while the Presbyterians and the Methodists and all the others could have bake sales or rummage sales or whatever they had back in those days. One delegate did argue that the Episcopal Church should be established because it was the *via media*, the middle way between too much religion (the evangelicals) and no religion at all. It was a fateful time for America.

Up stepped James Madison, quoting liberally from George Mason's "Declaration of Rights" and adding his own thoughts, which have been called "the most powerful defense of religious liberty ever written in America." Here's what he said: "The same authority which can establish Christianity to the exclusion of all other Religions may establish, with the same ease, any particular sect of Christians to the exclusion of all other sects."

He was just getting warmed up. Here's more: "Establishment corrupts piety. What have been its fruits? More or less in all places, pride and indolence in the clergy, ignorance and servility in the laity, in both, superstition, bigotry and persecution."

Did he have an opinion? There's still more, hotter still: "In many instances, ecclesiastical establishments have been seen upholding the thrones of powerful tyranny. IN NO INSTANCE HAVE THEY BEEN SEEN AS THE GUARDIANS OF THE PEOPLE. "

Wow! Although he talked like a Twenty-First Century Episcopalian, he was considered to be and thought of himself as merely a Deist. God was the Creator of the universe, but God has left us pretty much on our own. No matter what he was considered to be or thought of himself as, he was the man whose truth was established. Religion was not.

Here we are today. The separation of church and state is dogma in America and should be. The question always is: Whose religion (or church) should have power over the state? And whose state (i.e. party or president or administration) should have power over religion (or church)? The answer: No one's. Ever. One good thing is that that separation preserves our roles as priests *and* prophets, never bought and paid for.

Those founders of our nation paid a high price for our independence and our democracy. Some of them were captured and tortured by the British. Some lost all their property. Some were killed while fighting in the revolution. "Their lives, their fortunes, their sacred honor" isn't just so much verbiage. It's an exact description of what happened to them. As for the religious freedom of which we're the heirs, we're free to be who we are. We're free to be Christians. We're free to be Episcopalian Christians. The only thing that prevents us from being all that we can be is our own lack of nerve.

In 1979, two hundred years after The Declaration of Independence, we Episcopalians got a new *Book of Common Prayer.* There was glee and there was moaning. What's wrong with the 1928 book? We love it! Well, nothing's wrong, except, in my opinion, one thing: a clear call to action. The *Book of Common Prayer* we now have – well – it started a revolution. I've been a deacon, priest and bishop for fifty-one years; and, beginning in 1979, I've seen our Church change right before my eyes, becoming more and more the Jesus Movement. It thrills me.

I refer, particularly, to the effects – and the consequences – of "The Baptismal Covenant" in the rite of "Holy Baptism." At the very end of the Covenant, there are two questions:

1. "Will you seek and serve Christ in all persons, loving your neighbor as yourself?"
2. "Will your strive for justice and peace among all people, and respect the dignity of every human being?"

That's asking something of us. Nobody said it would be easy. Every time, we have to face up to our inhibitions and our fears. However, it draws us more and more into the heart of Christ.

Two things we know, for sure, that Jesus said: "You shall love the Lord your God with all your heart and with all your soul and with all your mind and with all your strength and you shall love your neighbor as yourself" and "DO NOT BE AFRAID."

We're at liberty in this land to be who we are, Episcopalian Christians. So let's be who we are and take the rap or take the praise, whichever, and call it our sacred play.

The Rt. Rev. John S. Thornton
St. Martin's Episcopal Church
Lebanon, Oregon
July 3, 2016

# The Plumb Lines Of The Good Life

What preacher would pass up a chance to talk about Amos, the prophet? He's called a "minor" prophet only because *The Book of Amos* is shorter than those of the "major" prophets, Isaiah, Jeremiah and Ezekiel. Otherwise, *Amos* has affected Judaism and Christianity in a major way. Martin Luther King, Jr. wasn't the only American who read and memorized lines from *Amos*. But nobody ever believed it more than he did.

"I hate, I despise your feasts,
    and I take no delight in your solemn assemblies.
Even though you offer me burnt offerings and cereal offerings,
    I will not accept them,
and the peace offerings of your fatted beasts
    I will not look upon.
Take away from me the noise of your songs;
    to the melody of your harps I will not listen.
BUT LET JUSTICE ROLL DOWN LIKE WATERS,
    AND RIGHTEOUSNESS LIKE AN EVER-FLOW-
    ING STREAM."

Not much is known about Amos. He lived in Tekoa, ten miles south of Jerusalem, on the way down to the Dead Sea. He was a simple man. He tended a small flock of sheep and a small olive orchard and, let's say, worked as a rock mason. He probably had a wife and kids to support. That's it, pretty much. Oh, and we mustn't forget, he took Torah to heart. For him, it really was the way of salvation.

Amos wanted everybody to know that he was a laborer and not a professional prophet. His father wasn't a professional prophet and his grandfather wasn't a professional prophet. He wasn't from a family of professional prophets. They were all rubes from a village where nobody would go to find God. (There is one exception to that, however. Solomon did go down there to consult "the wise woman of Tekoa." That's another story.) So Amos didn't have any connections and hadn't mastered the lingo and was clueless about the protocols among the beautiful people of Jerusalem and Bethel. Just another rube popping off, it seemed.

There's no reason not to assume that, in spite of all the labor, Amos went to synagogue on Friday evenings and observed the Sabbath and all that. He was a good Jew. He must have thought about Torah all the time. He must have thought about the essential and sanctifying impulse of his ancestors in Caanan, to be, among all the people of the world, those "chosen" for righteousness. That's why all the popping off, all the prophesying. "We listen to Torah being read, but we don't hear it anymore," he growled. He became agitated and convicted and righteous and very, very vocal. And could he draw a crowd.

Up to Jerusalem and Bethel he went, that rube from Tekoa. Up to the beautiful people, up to the culture-makers and the culture-keepers; up to the satisfied and the proud; up to the lost souls who didn't feel lost at all, but found and favored by God. They were living a lie that they had been singled out by God, that they were special, that they were chosen for privilege and power. Forget duty and discipline and deference to that old document rolled up in a tabernacle. We go to all the festivals, they fumed. We offer the sacrifices, they puffed. We're doing just fine. Go back to where you came from, rube.

It was in the middle of the Eighth Century B.C.E., a good time in Israel and Judah. Stable government under Jeroboam II. Pretty good king as kings and goodness go. No wars going on. Foreign trade was rip-roaring. The rich were getting richer (and fatter and sassier and less and less religious-er). As Amos pointed out, they could afford to buy beds made of ivory (Amos 6:4). But, while the rich were getting richer, the poor were getting poorer. Tough luck, the rich said. If you had some money, you wouldn't be poor. So go get a job. What? Go get a job? Who's going to hire a widow or a leper? The rich were living in defiance of Torah. "For the poor will never cease from the land; therefore I command you, you shall open wide your hand to your brother, to the needy and to the poor, in the land" (Deuteronomy 15:11). "OPEN WIDE YOUR HAND TO YOUR BROTHER." They had lost all sense of brotherhood and sisterhood. It was everyone for himself/herself.

"You have forgotten who you are!!!" screamed Amos. "You've forgotten that you're the descendants of immigrants from Egypt." They had no land. They had no money. They had little food. They were *the poor*. The one thing they had was the smarts and a tireless toughness and the deep, deep sense – no, the command from God – that they belonged to each other, that they would give their lives for each other. So you'd better get back to that essential and sanctifying impulse of your ancestors – or, by God, it will all go to ruins, he prophesied. Amos' "unfavorable" rating was about sixty-five percent ("favorable" was fifteen percent, "no opinion" twenty percent).

Now we get to the Old Testament lesson for today, the "plumb line," the perfect metaphor. He was speaking from his experience as a rock mason. If you build a rock wall, he said, it has to be plumb, the whole thing, all the way along. If it isn't plumb, if it leans, even a little bit, it's going to fall over, sooner or later. Maybe not in your time or your children's time or your grandchildren's time, but it will fall over.

I interject that old line about "visiting the iniquity of the father's upon the children and the children's children, to the third and fourth generations." Who believes that? Well, I'll tell you who believes that. Anybody who has ever studied family systems believes that. Something gets into the family system and it doesn't get out for generations. The consequences of our actions, whether good or bad, go on and on and on.

So Amos dangled that plumb line in front of the beautiful people and said, "Israel isn't plumb. If you don't pay attention to Torah, if you forget God, one day you'll be in ruins."

Really? Really.

So what is it that keeps us plumb?

There's a story in the Talmud about two First Century Jewish sages, Rabbi Hillel and Rabbi Shammai, archetypal opposites. Rabbi Hillel was a "loose constructionist of the Law," tolerant and tender. Rabbi Shammai was a "strict constructionist," inflexible and demanding. In the story about them, a Gentile comes to them, saying that he might convert to Judaism if either of them could teach him the whole Torah while standing on one leg. Shammai is so provoked that he whacks the Gentile with a measuring rod. Hillel, standing on one leg, replies, "That which is hateful to you do not do unto another. This is the whole Torah. The rest is commentary. Go and study." (The "go and study" part is very important, by the way. After you've read Torah ten thousand times, you finally get it. Same with the gospels.)

So what is it that keeps us plumb, from collapsing as persons and as a society?

The Golden Rule does. (I'm standing on one leg now.) "Do unto others as you would have them do unto you."

Or, as Rabbi Hillel, put it: "Do not do unto others as you would not have them do unto you." (I did that while standing on one leg.)

The Two Great Commandments do. When Jesus was asked what the greatest commandments in the Law are, he replied, "You shall love the Lord your God with all your heart and with all your mind and with all your soul and you shall love your neighbor as yourself. On these two commandments hang all the Law and the prophets." (Easy. I said all that while standing on one leg.)

The Beatitudes do.

"**Blessed are** the poor in spirit, for theirs is the kingdom of heaven."

"**Blessed are** those who mourn, for they shall be comforted."

"**Blessed are** the meek, for they shall inherit the earth."

"**Blessed are** those who hunger and thirst for righteousness, for they shall be satisfied." (I could do the first four while standing on one leg.)

"**Blessed are** the merciful, for they shall obtain mercy."

"**Blessed are** the pure in heart, for they shall see God."

"**Blessed are** the peacemakers, for they shall be called the children of God."

"**Blessed are** those who are persecuted for righteousness' sake, for theirs is the kingdom of heaven." (I did the second four while standing on one leg.)

These are some of the plumb lines of the good life.

Here's another, from *Micah*. (I'm standing on one leg.) "What doth the Lord require of thee, but to do justice and to love mercy and to walk humbly with thy God?" Those (justice, mercy and humility) are also the plumb lines of the good life.

There are all kinds of doctrines and dogmas in the churches, and you can believe whatever gives meaning to your life as a follower of the Christ *and* whatever increases your capacity to love your neighbor and the world for which our Lord died. I'd advise you to forget all the rest. They aren't essential. Plumbed with those things that are essential for the good life, you won't fall over.

One last thing: You have to encounter exactly one dozen people before you encounter one who is religious these days. A decade or so ago, you had to encounter only five people before you encountered one who is religious. Welcome to the minority. You're now the "remnant," the robust and visionary and utterly necessary, if often lonely, remnant. Take heart. Through you, society may get plumb again.

People are watching you and, from you, are learning how to be. The old, old story is that the few save the many.

The Rt. Rev. John S. Thornton
St. Martin's Episcopal Church
Lebanon, Oregon
July 17, 2016

# All Is Vanity?

"Vanity of vanities, all is vanity...and striving after the wind."

— Ecclesiastes

The "Teacher," whoever he was – he called himself a king in Israel – could never have gotten a job as a motivational speaker. What's there to be motivated for? It's all vanity. "Vanity of vanities, all is vanity... and striving after the wind." I know, it's in the Bible and all that, but it doesn't make any claim on my life. It's as if I, believing that everything in the Bible had absolute authority, would say to you that everything you've worked for, everything you've poured your heart into over the years, isn't worth a hill of beans. That message might turn you into the quintessential sad sack. Think nothing, say nothing, do nothing. Get life over with, quickly. It's all a waste of effort anyway.

I was reading an article about the University of Chicago philosopher Martha Nussbaum in the July 25th issue of *The New Yorker*. In her book titled *Sex and Social Justice* (1999), she refers to Dante's *Inferno*, particularly to the part about, "the crowd of souls who mill around the vestibule of hell, dragging their banner now one way now another, never willing to set it down and take a stand on any moral or political question." There's nothing important enough to look like a damned fool for. There's nothing worth sacrificing and suffering for. "Vanity of vanities, all is vanity...and striving after the wind" anyway.

Or maybe it wouldn't turn you into a sad sack. Maybe it would just turn you into a hedonist and a sybarite. You'd be like that "rich man" in today's gospel (Luke 12:13-21). Got a bumper crop. Had to build a bigger grain bin — or two or three. Grain for sale every day for the coming year — or two or three. Money...money, money, money. "Relax," he said to his soul, "eat, drink, be merry." What the ...?

Back in the 1950s, I had an atheist friend — he was a good friend and a good man, who didn't have a clue as to how godly he was — who used to taunt me by singing a phrase from an old gospel song, off-key always, "We are sinking deep in sin...wheee!!" It was all a pretense. He wasn't anything like that rich man.

Anyway, whatever pleasures you can wring out of life would be life's highest values. It leads to solipsism and amorality and total indifference — and being, say, the life of the wake.

Or maybe it wouldn't turn you into a hedonist and a sybarite. Maybe you'd talk back to me, put a fight: "Thornton, you're nuts. 'Vanity of vanity, all is vanity...and striving after the wind' doesn't match anything we know about the good life. Everybody's life has to have meaning, meaning that keeps him/her alive in spite of everything, meaning that lasts and lasts and lasts, meaning that transcends death."

I'm sure you know that *Man's Search for Meaning*, Viktor Frankl's book, was checked out of the New York Public Library more than any other book during the second half of the Twentieth Century. It was originally published as *Trotzdem Ja Zum Leben Sagen (Nevertheless,*

*Say "Yes" to Life)* largely written while he was in one of the Nazi death camps, on paper he swiped from the camp office. I read it in the late 1950s in its first English translation, which was titled *From Death Camp to Existentialism.*

Frankl survived that death camp partly because, as a medical doctor, he was assigned to a clinic. He observed that some people, though apparently not terminally ill, would just sit down in a corner and die, while others, in spite of the inhumanity of it all, the brutality of it all, the hell of it all, would never give up or give in. Beyond those barbed wire fences was a future worth holding out for.

After the death camp was liberated, Frankl went back to Vienna, back to his practice of neurology and psychiatry. He developed what he called "Logotherapy" (meaning therapy). It's a surpassing meaning that holds you in life, even when others have the power to take it away from you. It's a surpassing meaning that defies the Devil, in the multitude of forms he may appear in your life.

(Back in the 1970s, a college president invited me to a dinner party at which Viktor Frankl was the honored guest. Before dinner was served, I sat on a couch next to Frankl. Right next to him. I actually touched him, the great man, whose greatness was refined as humility and kindness.)

It's evident that the majority of us are seeking meanings that will last and last and laugh at death. That's exactly why the Orthodox save their best jokes for the Holy Saturday, the eve of Easter, to share them with the whole congregation. The message is that the joke is on death. Christ is risen! There's no whimpering about "vanity of vanities, all is vanity...and striving after the wind." Just the opposite: you can't nail the goodness of God to a cross; you can't wrap the goodness of God in a shroud; you can't lay the goodness of God in a tomb and roll a stone against the entrance and station guards outside; it will burst out and roam and race through the world.

All of that refers to passages in the first and second chapters of Ecclesiastes. The third chapter is a little more subtle, but equally deleterious. It's an especially enticing – captivating – sentiment. You probably know the lines by heart – and may love them, too.

> "For everything there is a season,
> and a time for every matter under heaven;
> a time to be born, and a time to die;
> a time to plant, and a time to pluck up what is planted...
> (So far so good.)
> a time to kill (Kill? A time to kill?), and a time to heal;
> a time to break down, and a time to build up;
> a time to weep, and a time to laugh...
> (Et cetera, concluding with:)
> a time to love, and a time to hate;
> a time for war, and a time for peace."

Tell me where I can find "a time to hate" and "a time for war" in the gospels, will you? Tell me. None of that ever came out of the heart of Jesus, and only the most perverse Christians have ever put it into his mouth.

Back in the days when I was a parish priest in California, people would ask to have that passage read or sung at weddings or funerals.

Not having begun my recovery from people-pleasing, I'd let them have their way. And, as it was being read or sung, I'd cringe. It's in the Bible, but I don't like it, one bit. In my opinion there's an inference of inevitability in it...an inference of determinism in it...an inference of fatalism in it...an inference of death-wishing in it. A time for this and a time for that...a time for this and a time for that...a time for this and a time for that. It's as if the Creator of the Universe started the whole thing and it's never going to stop. A time for this and a time for that.... So where's our moral decision-making and our moral action in all this? Where's our individuality and our independence in all this? Where's our authenticity and our actualization in all this? What are we good for?

Often people – very decent and very devout and very lovable people – tell me about "God's plan" in and for their lives. I'm never sure what to say. I consider it a time for mellow affirmation, not interrogation or argumentation. I always keep in mind what Elwood P. Dowd, in the play *Harvey*, said: "My mother used to tell me that, in this life, you have to be very smart or very pleasant. I've decided to be very pleasant." Me too.

Honestly, what I know about "God's plan" can be put on a postage stamp. Well, maybe on a post card, whatever it would take for the Shema ("Hear, O Israel, the Lord your God is one Lord....") and the Great Commandments and the Ten Commandments and the Golden Rule and the Beatitudes and a couple of other things (say Micah's "What doth the Lord require of thee but to do justice and to love mercy and to walk humbly with thy God?"), in small print. Oh, of course, those words from the Cross: "Father, forgive them, for they know not what they do."

For me, the question is not "What is God's plan for my life?" The question is "What is my plan for God's life in my life? What exactly is it that I need to do to incarnate the goodness of God in my life? (Parenthetically, in our Anglican tradition, we're all in the process of "making a soul." We're not born with a soul, which we can either wreck or gild in the living of our lives. We're making our souls.) So what exactly is it that I need to do today and tomorrow and all of this week to incarnate the goodness of God?

Soren Kierkegaard, the Danish theologian, would say that "purity of heart is to will one thing." One – only one and always only one – thing. That one thing is the love of God and neighbor. That's not "striving after the wind." That's striving for the deepest kind of peace and the deepest kind of joy.

So that you won't lapse into pessimism about the human race, I want you to know that I see people incarnating the goodness of God all the time. And if I could follow you around for a day, I'd bet the farm that I'd see you do it too. Remember, you're better than you think you are and the meaning of your life can be as eternal as God's life is eternal.

The Rt. Rev. John S. Thornton
St. Martin's Church
Lebanon, Oregon
July 31, 2016

# Moses And Jesus

Mother Anne emailed me a couple of weeks ago, to tell me that she would put Moses on the cover of the bulletin. The Old Testament lesson would be from The Book of Exodus. I emailed her back, saying, "You can't go wrong with Moses." What preacher would miss the opportunity? So Moses it is. Or should I say, Mosheh it is. "Mosheh" was his Hebrew name.

So how did Mosheh get a Hebrew name? He was an Egyptian. Well, he was an Egyptian by adoption, but a Hebrew by birth. You know the story. You've known it since you were kids. As for why his adoptive mother, Pharaoh's daughter, allowed or chose the Hebrew name, nobody knows.

The Pharaoh was half-crazed over the population explosion among the Hebrew slaves. In his opinion, they just weren't working hard enough. They had too much time and energy left over for making little Hebrews. So he ordered the project managers to work them so hard that they'd fall asleep over supper and would have to be shoved out of bed in the morning. And, in case of war, they'd be too weary to take the side of the enemy. Nothing worked. Those Hebrew slaves just kept on being fruitful and multiplying. So the Pharaoh came up with the perfect solution: kill all the Hebrew baby boys. (Kill them the minute they came into the world. Get rid of a whole generation of Hebrew males; and, then, the Egyptian boys could marry Hebrew girls and, then, they'd have half-Egyptian, half-Hebrew babies and, then, if everything worked out eugenically, Hebrew would end up being a recessive gene.)

So the Pharaoh called in all the Hebrew midwives to lay out his plan: as soon as they saw that a Hebrew baby was a boy, they should smother him and make it look like an accident. They listened carefully, as, of course, one would around pharaohs and kings. They nodded in agreement, fingers crossed. But, of course, they had no intention of doing what he ordered. You can't turn midwives into contract killers. They're on the side of life, for goodness' sake. When it was brought to his attention that the plan wasn't working, he called the midwives back in — and was he mad! "You didn't do what I told you to do!" he bellowed. "Where have all these Hebrew baby boys come from?" The midwives had a plausible lie: those Hebrew women were so strong. They'd give birth to their babies before the midwives could get to them. By the time they did, the new moms were happily nursing the little guys. Evidently, the Pharaoh didn't know any better and reluctantly believed them. But he had a new plan; and, this time, every Egyptian was ordered to do it: Whenever they saw a Hebrew baby boy, they should nab it and heave it into the Nile. "Drown all those potential reproducers! Drown those potential soldiers on the side of the enemy! Drown every last one of those little buggers!" The Pharaoh wasn't half-crazed anymore; he was one hundred percent crazed.

It was at this time that a young man and a young woman of the tribe of Levi got married and, a while later, had a baby. Phew! A girl. As the years went by, they had more babies, all girls. Finally, however, they had a boy. They managed to keep him hidden for three months, but somebody snitched. The desperate mom had just enough time to make a little boat, starting with an ordinary papyrus basket, which she plastered with "bitumen and pitch." She put the baby in it; and when nobody was looking, she took the boat and the baby down to the Nile, hoping that, floating there among the bulrushes, her baby would escape sure death. She had one of her daughters stand guard, at a distance. (It didn't work out quite the way she had hoped.)

On a hot afternoon, the Pharaoh's daughter, with a dozen or so of her attendants, went down to the Nile to bathe. She wasn't even up to her knees when she heard this wailing. So she waded out to where the wailing was coming from and, by golly, there was a little baby in a homemade boat. And was he hungry! But did she sink the boat and drown the baby as her father had ordered? Not on your life. That young woman had a heart. According to Scripture, "she had pity on him." The baby's sister, who had been watching from a distance, stepped up and said, "Oh, may I see the baby?" "Sure." "What a cute baby! He looks Hebrew. Would you like me to find a Hebrew wet nurse?" "What a great idea. Thank you!" So she ran off to get her mom, Mosheh's mom, to be the wet nurse. Perfect. The mom was the wet nurse until he was weaned, all those formative months. So the baby survived and - can you believe this twist of fate? - became a member of Pharaoh's household. The Pharaoh became his adoptive grandfather, who, probably, thought Mosheh was the cutest kid in Egypt. What a story. It gets better.

The Hebrew kid grew up as a prince. Pharaoh's daughter had plans for him: he would become her father's successor, a pharaoh himself. According to the historian Josephus, Mosheh became a general of the Egyptian army and led the defeat of the Ethiopians. But the glory faded, quickly.

When Mosheh could no longer stand the way the Egyptian project managers and their goons were treating the Hebrew slaves, he murdered one of them with his bare hands and, with his bare hands, dug a grave for him in the sand. It was a volcano of wrath, fired by an inexplicable tenderness toward the slaves. He had to run for his life. The military hero had become Egypt's Most Wanted. Mosheh fled to the Land of Midian, the southeastern part of the Sinai Peninsula. He stayed there for a generation, until Egypt had pretty much forgotten him – and until there was a new Pharaoh.

In Midian, he met and married a Preacher's Kid named Zipporah. Her father, Jethro, was the priest of some cult and a man of some wealth. Mosheh went to work for him, herding sheep; so he became the general of a flock, no longer of an army. But, for his spiritual growth and education in leadership, that's exactly what he needed. He needed to prepare himself for something big, educated by sheep.

One day, while minding the flock, he had this life-changing, history-changing, world-changing vision and audition ("the burning bush"). He came upon a bush that was burning but not burning up. (Don't try to explain it; it's symbolism.) A voice commanded: "Stop! Take off your shoes! This is holy ground! I am the God of your fathers, of Abraham, Isaac and Jacob!" It got his attention. He was all ears. There's more: "Now you go back to Egypt and free my people."

"Go back to Egypt and tell Pharaoh to (the congregation shouts, "Let my people go!").

"Go back to Egypt and tell Pharaoh to (the congregation shouts, "Let me people go!").

So Mosheh went back to Egypt, and you know the rest of the story, the Exodus.

Mosheh went back to Egypt, to organize the Hebrew slaves and to confront the new Pharaoh. In one confrontation after another, Mosheh, first as an appeal, then as a threat, yelled, "Let my people go!" It took a whole series of natural disasters to persuade the Pharaoh to let the Hebrew slaves go, though he sent his army after them. At the Red Sea, there was the final disaster. At last the slaves were free, never again to be anybody's slave. Never again to be anybody's slave. Oh, and never to enslave anybody else. We are meant to be free.

The centuries went by. Then a descendant of Mosheh, Jesus of Nazareth, the Galilean rabbi, appeared. He too cried, in his way, "Let my people go!"

From town to town in lower Galilee he went. "He was praised by everyone," Luke says. They loved him, and he loved them back. Finally, he headed home, to Nazareth. He suspected it would be different, though he wasn't sure how different it would be.

On a Sabbath day, Jesus went to the synagogue, "as his custom was," it says. "He stood up to read," it says. The hazan (the attendant) handed him the Isaiah scroll. He unrolled it to what in our Bibles is Isaiah 61. (There were no chapters and verses back in those days.) It's the soliloquy of what we used to call "the Righteous Servant of Jehovah" or, simply, a "Servant Song." I read from the King James Version, which I prefer, not that the NRSB isn't a good translation.

"The Spirit of the Lord is upon me;
because the Lord hath anointed me
to preach good tidings to the poor;
he hath sent me to bind up the broken-hearted,
to proclaim liberty to the captives,
and the opening of the prison to them that are bound...."

You can imagine that some of the people were saying, "Oh, what a beautiful lesson" or "Oh, he reads so well" or "Oh, we're so glad he's home again." Then he handed the scroll back to the hazan and sat down. Then he stood up again and looked them all straight in the eye. "Today, this scripture has been fulfilled in your hearing."

"What?"

"Fulfilled...in you?"

"Just who do you think you are?"

"You must think you're God Almighty!"

"We know your dad."

"That is so arrogant."

"It's worse. It's blasphemous!"

They got more and more agitated and crazed, the way religious people do when someone points out that their religion is religion, not the love of God above all loves. Feeling murderously righteous, the men of the synagogue marched Jesus out to the place of execution. However, under the Roman occupation, they didn't have the right to execute anybody. So they probably settled for what was called "a rebel's beating," cursing, spitting, punching, kicking, that would make him repent of suggesting that he himself was the Righteous Servant of Jehovah. Bruised and bloodied, Jesus managed to escape.

That's what happens when, in a religious system, anybody's religious system, people are indoctrinated to believe that God is up there, not down here, that God is beyond, not within, that there is no such thing as the humanity of God.

The Gospel is that Jesus of Nazareth is "God with us." What was true of Jesus is true of us — or can be — as well. We want Jesus to be Superman and ourselves hardly more than worms. The Jesus I meet in the gospels would rebuke us.

Once, they tried to make him a king. He'd have no part of it. "My kingdom is not of this world."

Once, he was approached by two young men who were fighting over their inheritance. They addressed him, obsequiously, as "good teacher." He snapped, "No one is good, but God alone."

Once, unequivocally, he said, "You think I do great things, but you will do greater things than these."

He was talking about what should be the norm for those who follow him. The norm for Christians is to bring good news to the poor (of whom there are millions in America). The norm for Christians is to bind up the broken-hearted (in our families, among our friends or anyone whose eyes bespeak sorrow or defeat). The norm for Christians is to proclaim liberty to the captives (and who is not a captive to the things that hurt both body and soul?) and the opening of the prison to them that are bound (all those who are innocent of crimes for which they have been sentenced – and may God bless the Innocence Project – and those imprisoned for non-violent crimes, in a country that incarcerates a greater percentage of its citizens than any country in the world).

The norm for Christians is to live as Jesus lived, to believe and to act as though

"The Spirit of the Lord is upon me;
because the Lord hath anointed me
to preach good tidings to the poor;
he hath sent me to bind up the brokenhearted,
to proclaim liberty to the captives,
and the opening of the prison to them that are bound...."

That, Jesus showed us, is how the Divine becomes human – in you.

The Rt. Rev. John S. Thornton
St. Paul's Episcopal Church
Salem, Oregon
February 28, 2016

# I Have Called You By Name

Let me tell you something about ancient Babylon. The Greeks considered it one or even two of the Seven Wonders of the World, with its walls and "hanging gardens." So how did it get to be one or even two of the Seven Wonders of the World? Not least of all because of the Jews, from Judea. The King of Babylon, Nebuchadnezzar, was a canny king. He had an army that couldn't be stopped. He had charioteers, swordsmen, archers by the thousands and a supply chain that stretched from Babylon to anywhere, to make conquest easy. That canny king had his eye on some of the smartest people in the world, the Jews, from Judea. "Go get them," he ordered the commander of his army, "and bring them back to Babylon. I need them." The year was, the scholars say, 597 BCE. He didn't need laborers; he had laborers. He needed the intelligentsia: doctors, lawyers, teachers, bankers, architects, engineers, artists, entrepreneurs. People like you. "Treat them nicely," he said. "Those people are like gold." Nebuchadnezzar didn't want Babylon to be just one or even two of the Seven Wonders of the World; he wanted Babylon to be all seven. Having no choice, but with lots of promises, the Judean Jews got in line. There were about ten thousand of them, they estimate. It wasn't long before they settled in, in Babylon. Though in exile, life wasn't half bad for the Jews. In fact, it was darned good.

The Prophet Jeremiah stayed behind — or was ordered to stay behind. Nebuchadnezzar didn't want a lot of yapping thus-saith-the-Lord types hanging around. However, Jeremiah wrote to the exiles, to tell them to make the best of it *and* to pray for the welfare of Babylon (Jeremiah 52:3, if you care to look it up). Evidently, they did make the best of it, for fifty or sixty or even seventy years, as exiles.

When King Cyrus, Nebuchadnezzar's successor two removed, allowed the Jews to go back to Judea, many didn't. "Are you kidding?" they said. "We love it here. This is a great place to live." Such as they made Babylon the center of Judaism in the ancient world.

Through most of the years of exile most of the Jews had a hankering for their homeland, Judea, Jerusalem in particular. No matter how well things were going in Babylon, their hearts weren't there. Hence the deep pain voiced in Psalm 137.

"By the waters of Babylon we sat down and wept,
    when we remembered you, O Zion.

As for our harps, we hung them up
    on the trees in the midst of the land.

For those who led us away captive asked us for a song, and
our oppressors called for mirth:
    "Sing us one of the songs of Zion."

How shall we sing the Lord's song
    upon an alien soil?"

Do you ever feel that you're an exile in your own land? By the waters of Eugene, do you ever sit down and weep? Well, that's maybe too theatrical. However, there must be moments when you feel out of place or left behind or useless. There must be moments when you feel like an alien. The feeling comes and goes but rarely stays, to depress you. Still, it does come. Often, however, there are so many compensations that we deny ever feeling that way. Life's good, at least okay. There's no point in complaining. Yet, by the waters of Eugene, we still can't sing the song we're asked or told to sing. Our hearts just aren't full of music.

That happened to me last Thursday morning. Jan and I had picked up a load of firewood a few miles outside of Albany and decided to go on into town, to Starbucks by the Fred Meyer store, to get some tea and *The New York Times*. With tea in hand, we sat down at a table and, there on the front page, was an article that read "After Mass Shootings, Some on Wall St. See Gold in Gun Makers." Since 2009, shares of Smith & Wesson and Sturm, Ruger & Company have increased more than 900 percent. Sales are up, prices are up, so shares are up. Whenever there's a mass murder, people buy more guns. When the President speaks about any kind of gun regulation, people buy more guns. (*The Register Guard* had the perfect Mike Luckovich cartoon that day. Two old duffers are sitting on a sofa, listening to the radio. The date on the calendar overhead is January 1, 1968. From the radio comes a voice: "Beginning today, all vehicles must have seatbelts...." One duffer says to the other, "They're coming for our cars!!!") Could it be that we're trying to make our escape into the captivity of doubt, suspicion and fear?

(I recognize that the majority of gun-owners – that includes me, with my single-barrel, single-shot 12-gauge shotgun, which I occasionally fire into the air to scare the deer away from the fruit orchard – are reasonable, responsible, self-restrained people, though some people aren't. It's not that easy to tell who's which.)

Then I read, in *The American Scholar*, in an article titled "Medication Nation," "that our increasing reliance on drugs – prescribed, over-the-counter, illegal, and ordered online like pizza – suggests that we have a deeper problem." Of course, there is pain, physical and psychic, to be treated mercifully. There's also the pain of living life without great, surpassing meaning. Hence the drugs.

Then I read, in *The Register Guard,* that we're headed toward a "cashless society." I hope not in my lifetime. I've been counseling people for the past forty-five years to use cash and never or hardly ever credit cards, except in emergencies or when there's no choice, as when you purchase airline tickets. In this digital collectivization of persons, there has to be more than a modicum of privacy.

Not only do I feel like an old fogey, I often feel like an alien in the land of my birth.

You people are so polite. Nobody is going stand up and say, "Thornton, stop your whining."

But that's exactly what Isaiah did. "So," he said, "you're not in Jerusalem any more; you're in Babylon. Stop your whining. This is where you live now. It's up to you how you live. It's not as if the God of Abraham, Isaac and Jacob has forsaken you."

Listen to this:

"Thus says the Lord,
    he who created you, O Jacob,
    he who formed you, O Israel:
Do not fear, for I have redeemed you;
    I have called you by name, you are mine."

Then he goes on to say, "I'd trade Egypt and Ethiopia and Seba and all the rest of the world for you, I love you so much."

Do you have the sense – or, on the basis of all the graces you've been given over the years, the knowledge – that you are loved by God? Or, as Jesus said, "Every hair on your head is counted."

I don't mean that you're loved more than anyone else. I mean that you have been loved into the belief that "nothing can separate you from the love of God" (St. Paul). I mean that you have been loved into such security that you're free to love others, including those who don't love you now and may never.

It's in that sense, to use Isaiah's words, that you've been "created," "formed," "redeemed," "ransomed," that sends you into an imperfect world, a troubled, dangerous world, into a world in which you, like me, often feel like an alien. Confidently and fearlessly, you find a way to live in this old world in a new way. You may not see the results in your lifetime, as Reinhold Niebuhr warned – but your love is never wasted and is forever, deep down within you, "the joy of the Lord."

Isaiah gets the last word: "Do not fear...I have called you by name; you are mine."

YOU ARE MINE.

The Rt. Rev. John S. Thornton
St. Thomas Church
Eugene, Oregon
January, 10, 2016

# A Terrible Beauty

I want your help with this sermon. Whenever I say, "Therefore, we proclaim the mystery of faith," you say,

> CHRIST HAS DIED,
> CHRIST IS RISEN,
> CHRIST WILL COME AGAIN.

Say it. Say it a little more softly. Now say it very softly.

In a book titled *A Terrible Beauty,* James Carroll tells a story about himself – or, as we sometimes say – *on* himself. He is appalled by his behavior, and he is penitent.

At the time of the incident that he describes, he was a priest of the Roman Catholic Church. However, on this particular occasion, he wasn't in "clericals." He was free of all the symbols, free of the persona of a professional Churchman.

It all occurred on a subway train in Boston. He boarded and took a seat, the only available seat, next to a young woman. Though he strained not to notice, he *did* notice that she was, well, she was a knockout! And as the train rocked along, they rubbed against each other. As it stopped at stations, she slid into him; and as it lurched forward, he was thrown against her. With all that contact, his soul was crying out, "Chastity be damned!" And he could feel her eyes enfolding him. When he did quickly glance at her, she was looking straight at him. He tried to distract himself by focusing on the maps of the subway system and the billboards as the train rocketed past. Finally, the man inside of him, the man he had suppressed for so many years, spoke up and said (to him), She's going to ask you to have a drink with her...She's going to ask you to have dinner at her apartment...She's going to.... No longer able to constrain himself – or the man inside himself – he swung around and looked directly at her, directly into her shining eyes. And she was looking directly at him; and glowing with hopefulness, she said, "Are you a Christian?" And he, horrified and humiliated by his misperception of her, by his perversion of her innocence, said emphatically, "No!" At the next station, which wasn't his, he got up and bounded out, not only with the vision of this terrible beauty in his head, but with a vision of the terrible beauty of the God who knows him through and through.

To every encounter with the little brothers and sisters of Jesus, we bring ourselves...we bring all that we are and have been since our conception...we bring all that we are not yet as we grow "more and more into the likeness of Christ." And our reactions do vary wildly. As Gerard Manley Hopkins said, "For Christ plays in ten thousand places,/Lovely in limbs, and lovely in eyes not his...." But not all, unlike the young woman who rode the subway train with James Carroll, are lovely in limbs, lovely in eyes. Some are not lovely at all – though the least lovely could be the *one*, as Isaiah said, the Holy One of God, who "has neither form nor comeliness that we should look upon him, no beauty that we should desire him." And so to each encounter we bring our confusion and, to use a New Testament word, we bring our "fear." Yet we know that the gospel of the Risen Christ is "Do not be afraid!" We are commanded never to be afraid of meeting others heart to heart, because we will meet God in them.

All human beings bear the image of God. But who would not confess that it is easier to see God in some persons than in others? Only the saints have been able to do this beyond all evidence. St. Francis of Assisi saw God in a leper and Mother Theresa of Calcutta sees God in the faces of those who are dying on the streets. And as for us, well, we must pray to have the Beatific Vision, which is not to see God, but to see as God sees. And God sees in each one of us "a terrible beauty." Oh, that we could see it in each other with the eyes of the heart. And we will.

In today's gospel, St. Matthew repeats Jesus' parable of the ten bridesmaids, five of whom are called "foolish" and five of whom are called "wise." This is not some kind of formula. Jesus is not dividing humankind into two categories, the foolish and the wise. People are always trying to do that, though often with good reason. Psychologist Eric Fromm divides human beings into "creators" and "destroyers." Psychoanalyst Viktor Frankl divided them into "the decent" and "the unprincipled." Among Episcopalians, I have been able to identify two categories: (1) those who, first, stand up, then try to find the page in the Hymnal and (2) those who, first, try to find the page in the Hymnal, then stand up. Beyond that, Episcopalians are far too complex for me. The best you can do is love them as they are.

The difference between folly and wisdom, according to St. Matthew, according to Jesus, is readiness, is ever-readiness for the coming of the bridegroom, for the coming of *the* bridegroom, the Christ. He is the Lord of surprises...who came as a baby born in a stable in Bethlehem of Judea...who came as a laborer (most say a carpenter, but anyone who thinks about the parables knows he had to have been a farmer)...who came as a self-taught rabbi who loved God and the Word of God so much that he became the flesh of that Word, of God Godself....who came as a "king" riding on an donkey at a time so untimely that it could only have been *the* time...who came crowned with brambles and clothed only in the purple of cold and dying flesh as he hung on the cross...who came with wounded feet and wounded hands and wounded side into that place where the disciples *for fear* were hiding, huddled, to embrace them and to breathe into their wounded souls the unutterable peace of forgiveness...and who will come again and again and again as you come into my life and as I come into yours with an unconditional love.

Therefore, we proclaim the mystery of faith,

CHRIST HAS DIED,
CHRIST IS RISEN,
CHRIST WILL COME AGAIN.

But, you say, "How can we be ready?" Dietrich Bonhoeffer puzzled over this too. "How can we be ready," he asked, "for that for which we can't be ready?" How can we be ready for the total surprise of grace? And the answer, the only answer, is the answer of St. John the Baptist: "Prepare the way of the Lord." Prepare a way into your hearts and through your hearts into the lives of others.

Over the years, I have heard people say, I've given up looking for the Messiah. I understand, but it makes me sad that any Christian would give up looking. Have we not seen marvelous things in each other since coming to this Convention? Did we not recognize something wondrous in those who received the Bishop's Crosses last night?  And is there not more, infinitely more, to be seen in the little brothers and sisters of Jesus today?  Do we not expect to behold a terrible beauty?

J. D. Salinger's *Frannie and Zooey* is a book that has been important to me since the early sixties.  In it, there are two main characters: Frannie and Zooey.  But there are more: their mother, a simple and saintly woman who sees little difference between a bowl of chicken soup and the Body and Blood of Christ; their dead brother, Seymour; and Professor Tupper, who has gotten Frannie hooked on, and nearly crazed by, "The Jesus Prayer" ("Lord Jesus Christ, Son of God, have mercy on me, a sinner.").

Frannie and Zooey and Seymour were all very precocious children.  Seymour was particularly precocious spiritually.  They were the stars of a radio program called "Wise Child," on which they answered difficult questions about geography, history, literature, mathematics, anything.  Though it was all done in a radio booth, Seymour would bathe, put on his Sunday best, and carefully comb his hair as if the most important person in the world might see him.  When he got into the booth at the radio station, he would close his eyes tightly and, breathing deeply, would visualize one person out there in the radioland.  That person was an old woman, fat, veiny, with stringy hair and broken teeth and empty, empty eyes.  She was the least attractive person he could imagine, and he gave her a name.  The name he gave her was "Christ."  She had neither form nor comeliness that he should look upon her, no beauty that he should desire her.  Yet look upon her he did.  With all his heart, he desired her joy.  His answers to the difficult questions sent in to the program were all an offering to her.

As we prepared for this Convention, more than one person said to me, "Wait 'til next year. The honeymoon will be over." I take it that the honeymoon will be over for *me*. That doesn't frighten me in the least, but it does make me think. What that says to me is that the time is coming when, as the Jungians say, we will withdraw our projections and, once again, behold each other as diminished persons. What that says to me is that we will have given up on the unconditional love. What that says to me is that we will have accepted failure. Never...never...never. When the Church finally takes itself seriously, as the Bride of Christ, the honeymoon will never be over. Our life together will be a sign of that perfect unity which exists among Father, Son, and Holy Spirit.

We have a history with each other. Most of it is good history. Some of it isn't. It doesn't matter, ultimately. All our sins have been forgiven. As of this moment, we begin a new history as a new people. Now God is appealing to us to look at each other innocently and to listen to each other naively and to expect the Risen Christ to rise in our hearts. You never know, you just never know when, suddenly, you will experience the *sophia*, the wisdom of God, in "one of the least of these"...when you will experience the *hilarotees*, the hilarity of God, in the cheerfulness or humor of one who sits across from you at table...when you will experience the *dunamis*, the power of God, in the strength of a truly virtuous person...when you will experience the *charis*, the grace of God, in the spontaneous giving and forgiving of one who loves you...when you will experience the *eucharistia*, the thankfulness of God, in someone's heartfelt gratitude for your doing something for which you never expected recognition, praise or reward...when you will experience the *agapee*, the holy love of the holy God, in the steadfast love of husband and wife, of parents and children, of partners and friends.

Get ready. Be ready, always. Christ is coming into our lives. Therefore, we proclaim the mystery of faith,

CHRIST HAS DIED,
CHIST IS RISEN,
CHRIST WILL COME AGAIN.

The Rt. Rev. John S. Thornton
Preached at the 23rd Annual Convention of
The Episcopal Diocese of Idaho
Pocatello, Idaho
November 1991

Made in United States
Troutdale, OR
06/15/2025